Clairvoyance, Thought Transference, Auto Trance, and Spiritualism

L.W. DE LAURENCE

COSIMOCLASSICS

NEW YORK

Clairvoyance, Thought Transference, Auto Trance, and Spiritualism
Cover © 2007 Cosimo, Inc.

For information, address:

Cosimo, P.O. Box 416
Old Chelsea Station
New York, NY 10113-0416

or visit our website at:
www.cosimobooks.com

Clairvoyance, Thought Transference, Auto Trance, and Spiritualism was
originally published in 1916.

Cover design by www.kerndesign.net

ISBN: 978-1-60206-661-8

CONTENTS

CONTENTS

Preface

This work is intended to cover such intensely interesting subjects as *Thought-Transference, Mental Telepathy, Clairvoyance, Psychometry, Hypnotism* and *Spiritualism.*

Thought-reading is duly considered and explained. A clear distinction is drawn between *Musculation,* or *Muscle* and *Mind-Reading;* and although these pages are not confined to *Thought-Reading,* as generally understood by the public, the subject itself, and as an entertainment, have been most fully dealt with.

During the past decade, psychological subjects have, in a remarkable way, arrested public attention. *"Mesmerism"* and *"Spiritualism"* are popular subjects with editors and magazine writers. Whatever the real causes—a greater influx of the spiritual from *"the state of the dead,"* or from a reaction in the minds of men against the purblind materialism of our scientific leaders—it is hard to say. Possibly these and other causes have been at work. One thing is certain, for good or ill, the majority of thinking men and women of the age are not only interested in, but are actually searching for evidence of *"embodied spirit."* Hence we find men of science, journalists, and even professed materialists and secularists, who, a few years ago, could scarcely speak of these subjects in the ordinary language of courtesy, confess now not only their belief, but are going to the other extreme of advocating, what as yet, they have failed to fully grasp.

A few years ago *"The British Parliament of Science"* was nothing if not materialistic. The leading

5

savants of the day declared "*all was matter, no matter what.*" Consequently, man was the highest product of protoplasm, and his *only* destiny the grave. The change has been great indeed, when one of its most brilliant members, *Professor Oliver Lodge, D.Sc., F.R.S., British Association at Cardiff, 1891*, in his address said:

"It is familiar that a thought may be excited in the brain of another person, transferred thither from our brain by pulling a suitable trigger; by liberating energy in the form of sound, for instance, or by the mechanical act of writing, or in other ways. A prearranged code, called language, and a material medium of communication, are recognized methods. May there not, also, be an *immaterial*, perhaps an ethereal, medium of communication? Is it possible that an idea can be transferred from one person to another by a mental process such as we have not yet grown accustomed to, and know practically nothing about? *In this case I have evidence. I assert I have seen it done, and am perfectly convinced of the fact; many others are satisfied of the truth, too.* It is, perhaps, a natural consequence of the community of life or family relationship running through all living beings. *The transmission of life may be likened in some ways to the transmission of magnetism, and all magnets are sympathetically connected, so that, if suitably suspended, a vibration from one disturbs others, even though they be distant 92,000,000 miles.* It is sometimes objected that, granting *Thought-Transference* or *Telepathy* to be a fact, it belongs more especially to lower forms of life, and that as the cerebral hemispheres develop we become independent of it; that what we notice is the relic of a decaying faculty, not the germ of a new and fruitful sense, and that progress is not to be made by studying or alluding to it. As well might the objection be urged against a study of embryology. *It may, on the other hand, be an indication of a higher mode of communication, which shall survive our temporary connection with ordinary matter.* The whole region is unexplored territory, and it is conceivable that matter may react on mind in a way we can at present only dimly imagine."

Thought-Transference and *Telepathy* may, indeed, be an indication of a higher mode of communication between human beings after we have severed our temporary connection with matter. Whether or not, the hope should repay our study. I have in the following pages to briefly define and illustrate what these phases of communication are.

Double and *Psychic Consciousness, Clairvoyance,* natural and induced; *Psychometry,* its natural and leading features as a spiritual faculty; *Thought-Transference, visions, dreams,* and their *portents,* are in turn briefly dealt with, in order to extract therefrom some evidence of the action of the human *soul.*

Modern Spiritualism is referred to, in so far as *Thought-Reading* is likely to throw any light upon its psychological phases, as well as on its physical phenomena.

While attempting to cover so much ground my difficulty was not what to write, but what not to write, the materials at my disposal being so abundant. Much has been cut down to get the whole within reasonable compass. Nevertheless, I know the reader will find this book a most valuable work on the above subject.

L. W. DE LAURENCE.

Clairvoyance And Thought-Transference

CHAPTER I.

SOMNAMBULISM

AND PSYCHIC PHENOMENA

Before entering upon the subject of "CLAIRVOYANCE
AND THOUGHT-TRANSFERENCE"—or rather, range of
interesting subjects grouped under this title—it is pro-
posed to deal briefly with the *"Key"* to the whole.
which is to be found in the revelations of man's inner
life, *soul-life and character,* presented by *Somnambulism* and *Trance,* whether natural or induced.

The use of a few simple terms having a well-defined
meaning will help the reader and prepare him for the
more careful study of the psychic side of human life.

The somnambulistic and trance states may be
divided, for the convenience of examination, into the
Hypnotic, or state of hypnosis; the *Mesmeric,* or somnambulistic; and the Psychic, or lucid somnambulistic—
or briefly, the *Hypnotic, Mesmeric* and *Psychic* states.

The operator is the controlling agent, *Hypnotist,* or
Mesmerist; in spiritualism, *the guide or control.*

The sensitive is the subject, the percipient, psychic,
patient, or person who passes into the hypnotic, mesmeric, or trance states, etc.

Hypnosis is the term used for the hypnotic state arti-
ficially induced by the agent. *Hypnosis* is the lowest

rung of the ladder; the psychic or soul state the highest. The intermediate phases, as indicated in conscious or sub-conscious conditions of life, are innumerable and not readily classified. Still, the states mentioned will give a favorable insight to the whole. In hypnosis, physical rather than mental phenomena are evolved; *anæsthesia,* or non-sensitiveness to pain, is more or less present. The senses of smell and hearing are partially exalted, and the sensitive may be partially or wholly unconscious.

The mesmeric state is the term frequently used to denote ordinary artificial somnambulism. It is actually the higher or more perfect form of hypnosis. The senses in this state are more fully submerged, and the mental faculties are more fully exalted, than in hypnosis.

The psychic state, as the mesmeric, relates to the mental, and hypnosis to the more physical, so does the psychic state refer to that class of extraordinary somnambulism in which the mental and the spiritual gifts transcend in character and power those of the foregoing states. In this state the higher phenomena of lucid somnambulism, clairvoyance, and thought-transference are manifested more perfectly than in any other.

The *Hypnotic,* the *Mesmeric,* and the *Psychic* states indicated are frequently interlinked in manifestation. The sensitive may pass from the first to the last without apparent gradation. It is well to keep these divisions in thought, so that in practice no one will be content with the *lower* where it is possible, by wise and judicious observations and operations, to induce the higher.

To make the matter still more clear, in hypnosis and in the mesmeric state all phenomena may be said to be induced through and by the influence and the direction of the operator. Not that he produces the effects as they are exhibited by the sensitive, but they are brought about through the agency of his suggestions or operations.

In the psychic state this is not always the case. The influence of the operator may at times be almost *nil*. The operator will find it best—when the sensitive is in a high lucid state—to become an observer and a learner, and no longer continue the *rôle* of director.

In the psychic state, the soul-powers, so often submerged in ordinary life, transcend in a remarkable manner. The senses are completely suspended and the mind exalted to such a degree, a clearly defined supersensuous condition is reached. Whether this stage or condition is induced by fasting, prayer, disease, or by mesmeric agencies, matters little. In it we find the key to the seership, and the clairvoyance, and the prophetic utterance, and the mystic powers attributed to and exercised by prophet, and seer, and sybil in the past. By the investigation of the phenomena evolved by the psychic state we are enabled to understand something of man's soul or spiritual nature, apart from the phenomena induced by pathological conditions of brain and body.

The foregoing view presented of mesmeric conditions may be very different from that which medical men may glean from hypnotic practice with hysterical and lobsided patients, and certainly not the views which the general public are likely to gather from seeing a number of paid "subjects" knocked about a music hall stage by an ignorant showman.

From the roughest to the finest, from matter to spirit, from hypnosis to the psychic state, we find enough to arrest attention and give a high degree of seriousness and earnestness to our investigation. We stand on the threshold of soul, and the place where we stand is holy ground. We find, as is the physical, mental, and spiritual characteristics of the operator, *plus* those of the sensitive or sensitives, so will be the nature of the phenomena evolved.

It will be observed some subjects never get beyond the first state, or hypnosis; others that of the second, or mesmeric. All sensitives, in keeping with their temperamental and mental developments (as revealed by phrenology and psychometry), are better adapted for one class of phenomena than that of others.

It may be further observed that the foregoing states may be self-induced or, directly and indirectly, the product of "spirit-control," drugs, or bodily disease. Hypnosis, we must bear in mind, although not unlike the mesmeric state, has no more relation to that condition than sleep produced by an exhaustive walk or a dose of laudanum is like natural or healthy sleep. Indeed, hypnosis is not properly a condition of sleep. In the majority of cases the sensitive is never wholly unconscious. It is rather a state in which there is a temporary perversion or subordination between brain impressions and consciousness. The sensitive in hypnosis is often less intelligent than in the normal or waking state.

For various reasons the state of hypnosis may be recognized as that state in which the mind is subjected to certain abnormal conditions of the body, notably of the brain, spinal cord, and indirectly of the circulation, induced by certain means determined upon by the operator. The mental condition in this state is one of almost pure automatism, in which hallucination or sense illusions are more or less present.

Great and serious are the responsibilities of those who bring about the state of hypnosis. Every thought and feeling, of whatever kind, infused in this state, like seed, will take root and germinate, and finally bud into action in the daily or waking consciousness, and determine unconsciously for the sensitive the character of his life. HYPNOTISM is neither for indiscriminate *use, nor is hypnosis to be induced as a plaything for the thoughtless—medical or lay. At the same time, in the hands of the thoughtful, its educative value is most important, for, if the operator is well poised, and feels that, he can impart higher thoughts and strengthen the *will of the sensitives by the twofold agencies of impressionability and suggestion. This is something not to be despised. It is surely no degradation to be saved from evils one cannot overcome or resist, unless assisted by external aid, even though that help can only come by submitting to hypnotism.*

In hypnosis the outer brain of convoluted grey matter is most affected, being more or less denuded of arterial and nervous stimuli. The power of conscious, intellectual, and abstract thought is reduced to a minimum. The organs of the central brain are differently influenced, as in inverse ratio the stimulation is increased. The eye is more susceptible to light, or the pupils may become dilated and fixed. The auditory sense is rendered more keen. The olfactory powers are intensified, and there is more or less insensibility of feeling. The powers of co-ordination and locomotion are preserved up to a certain stage, when these functions are disturbed, all power of voluntary movement ceases, lethargic and cataleptic symptoms supervene.

It was by observing, more particularly, hypnosis, Professor Heidenhain was led to aver *"inhibition"* actually accounted for all phases of hypnotism. This opinion has evidently been based on a limited number of cases. *"No inhibition,"* says Dr. Drayton, "however

---

* In this way evil habits, such as errotic mania, opium eating, dipsomania, etc., may be cured. When the strength of the vice and the deterioration of the brain and body are such as to undermine the will of the patient, hypnotism, properly employed, may be used and recognized as a powerful and legitimate curative agent.

ingeniously applied, will explain all the phenomena of magnetism. If the personal consciousness, the individualty, of the subject has been lost, and his state is that of automatism, or rather that of an involuntary actor, certainly his cerebral functions operate in a manner entirely distinct from that which is characteristic in his ordinary state. The inhibition relates to his common order of conduct mentally, while the super-sensitivity and extraordinary play of faculty that he may exhibit, indicate a higher phase of sensory activity, more free or harmonious co-ordination of the cerebral functions. The brakes are off, hence the phenomena that are frequently observed in the somnambulist, and awaken wonder, because so much out of keeping with what is known of his common life."

Here we find doctors—experts in hypnotism or mesmerism—agree to differ. They agree in this, albeit not expressly stated, they are alike positive and decided in their views, and certainly *without being positive, there is no possible success as an operator.*

The mistake they make evidently arises in confounding the two states, *hypnosis* and the *mesmeric*, one with the other. There is no super-sensitivity, or extraordinary play of faculty in hypnosis, whatever there may be in the mesmeric state. They are similar, in that they may be both induced by the reduction of the activity of the cerebral cortex.

In hypnosis the mind slumbers and dreams. The dream-life appears as substantial to the sensitive as the waking life. The life creations, thus dreamed of, are acted upon, whether they arise from suggestion or other causes.

In the mesmeric state the senses slumber, and the mind awakens to a fuller enfranchisement of existence, and to the exhibition of mental and spiritual powers not hitherto suspected.

In the lower stages the increased power of the senses

is to be found in the *intense concentration* of effort, brought about from the fact that the subject's attention is, and his whole energies are, directed in one line of action of thought, to the exclusion of mind or brain activity in other directions. Hence all efforts are centred in the direction suggested by the operator, or self induced, as suggested by the "dominant idea."

The sensitive exhibits powers of mind and ability of thought which were not noticeable in the ordinary waking condition. Not because he really possesses greater powers of mind or body, but because of the lack of concentration in the waking state. By this concentration of direction, so called abnormal feats of strength are performed, rigidity of structure brought about, and other characteristics not peculiar to common life. In a higher sense, we see the sensitive passing from this condition of concentration of one-idea-ism to a spiritual state, in which the phenomena exhibited are no longer the product of self-dethronement and of suggestion. Higher still, we see the soul reign supreme. The sensitive possesses a clear consciousness of what is transpiring at home and abroad, according to the direction of his psychic powers.

In the psychic state—the more perfect trance state or control—the whole mind becomes illumined; past, present, and future become presentable to the mind of the lucid somnambulist as one great whole. This higher stage may be reached through the simple processes of manipulation, and passes as suggested in my little work, "How to Mesmerise."

In the mesmeric state the sensitive passes from the mere automatism of the earlier stages of hypnosis to the distinct individuality indicated above, although still more or less influenced or directed by his controller or operator into the line of thought and train of actions most desired.

The difference between the *Hypnotic* and *Mesmeric*

states should now be very clear. In the former the sensitive has no identity, in the latter his identity is preserved in a clearly individualised form throughout the whole series of abnormal acts. Whenever the sensitive enters this condition his personal consciousness is most apparent in the middle and higher stages.

In fact, in the mesmeric state, it is very stupid for some operators to ask the sensitive, *"Are you asleep?"* It may be understood what is meant, yet the question is absurd from the standpoint of an intelligent observer. *The sensitive is never more awake.* The higher the state the greater the wakefulness and lucidity of the inner or soul life.

The Sixth Sense.

In the *"Mesmeric State"* we see developed the *"magnetic sense"*—or *"sixth sense."* It is a gift of supersensitiveness. *To my mind it is the enfranchisement of the soul, the human ego—in proportion as the dominance of the senses is arrested.*

In blindness, it has been noticed how keen the sense of touch becomes. I have also noticed the keen sensitiveness of facial perception enjoyed by some of the blind, by which they are enabled to perceive objects in the absence of physical sight. In the mesmeric state we see a somewhat analogous mental condition. As the peculiar sense of the blind is developed by extra concentration of the mind in the direction of facial perception, so is *"the sixth sense"* developed by concentration of direction, as well as by the condition of sensitiveness induced by the mesmeric state.

This newly recognised sense, *"the sixth sense,"* not only answers the purpose of sight and hearing, but transcends all senses in vividness and power. Materialists, no longer able to ignore the phenomena of somnambulism and trance, and compelled to admit man's avenues of knowledge in this life were not confined to the recognised five senses, are good enough to give him a *"sixth sense,"* even while they deny him a soul. In the same way, no longer able to deny the existence of mesmerism, they now admit it to consideration—re-baptised as hypnotism. The phenomena being admitted, we will not quarrel over the names by which they are called.

PSYCHIC-CONSCIOUSNESS

As we advance in our investigations we find in the higher conditions of these states a double or treble consciousness or memory. The higher including and overlapping the lower. Thus the consciousness of the hypnotic state includes that of the waking state, while the memory of the waking state possesses no conscious recollection of what has taken place in hypnosis, and so on, each stage has its own phases of consciousness. The memory of the sensitive, under influence, over lapping and including the memory of ordinary or normal life.

Strange as it may appear, there are no phenomena which have been evolved in any of these abnormal conditions of life, which have not been observed again and again in ordinary or normal life, as well authenticated instances of dreams, warnings, and telepathy testify.

In dreams and visions of the night, spirits have manifested themselves to man in all ages. In other words, the soul (in sleep and analogous states to somnambulism and trance) comes more in touch with the sub-conscious or soul sphere of thought and existence. At times there is an inrush from that sphere into man's present conscious state, by which he knows of things which could not otherwise be known. Of dreams, my space will not admit more than occasional reference. I may mention as a case in point the dream of Mrs. Donan, wife of the livery stableman from whom Dr. Cronin hired his horse in *Chicago.* *A week before Dr. Cronin was murdered this lady had a dream-vision, and dreamt he was barbarously murdered, and saw in a vision the whole terrible scene.* This dream was a means, first, of forewarning the doctor, and second, of leading to the detection of the miscreants.

Of premonitions, an incident reported in the *Register* of Adelaide, will suffice: "Constable J. C. H. Williams has reported to headquarters that he had an unpleasant experience at about midnight on Monday. He was on duty at the government offices in King William Street, and while standing at the main entrance he had a presentiment that he was in danger, and walked away a few steps. Scarcely had he moved from the spot, when a portion of the cornice work at the top of the building fell with a crash on the place where he had been standing. The piece of plaster must have weighed fully a stone, and had it struck Williams the result would doubtless have been fatal. A passer-by saw the constable a few minutes after, and his scared looks and agitated manner clearly showed that his story was true." Concerning telepathy, Mrs. Andrew Crosse, the distinguished widow of the famous electrician, relates in *Temple Bar* an anecdote about the late Bishop Wilberforce, to the effect, the Bishop was writing a dry business letter one day, when a feeling of acute mental agony overcame him and he felt that some evil had befallen his favourite son, a midshipman in the navy. The impression was correct. On that very day the lad, who was with his ship in the Pacific, had been wounded and nearly bled to death. When this was told Hallam, the historian, he replied that a very similar thing had happened to himself. A few cases are noted further on. Some persons would repudiate *all* such incidents as accidents or coincidences; while others would fly to the extreme, and declare all such are the result of "spirit control"—that is, some disembodied but friendly spirit projected the dream, conveyed the warning, or telepathically despatched the news. But we must never forget news has to be received as well as despatched. Consequently, we, as embodied spirits, must possess psychic consciousness.

I believe that *much* of the phenomena, directly and indirectly attributed to disincarnate spirit control, are traceable to *no other source* than the powers of our own embodied spirits, as revealed by the facts of somnambulism and trance, and this is the opinion of all intelligent spiritualists.

"Because," says Mr. G. H. Stebbins, a prominent investigator of modern spiritualism in the United States, "a person quotes from books he never saw, or *tells of what he never knew* in any external way, that is not final proof that he is under an external spirit control. *Psychometry* and *Clairvoyance* may sometimes solve it all."

"I hold," says Mr. Myers, "that telepathy and clairvoyance do, in fact, exist—*Telepathy,* a communication between incarnate mind and incarnate mind, and perhaps between incarnate minds and minds unembodied; clairvoyance, a knowledge of things terrene which over-passes the limits of ordinary perception, and which, perhaps, achieves an insight with some other than terrene world."

These are the cautious admissions of eminent investigators in psychical research.

DOUBLE OR SUB-CONSCIOUSNESS.

"*There are two sets,*" says Dr. Brown-Sequard, "a double state of mental powers in the human organism, essentially differing from each other. The one may be designated as ordinary conscious intelligence; the other, a superior power, which controls our better nature."

J. Balfour Brown, in his *"Medical Jurisprudence,"* says: "In no case of pure somnambulism, waking consciousness of the individual knows anything of the sleeping consciousness. It is as if there were two distinct memories."

This double consciousness, memory, or sub-state of mental powers, is another but lower phase of psychic-consciousness, and is sometimes exhibited by accidents, and also by disease.

Dr. Abercromby relates the case of a boy, four years old who was trepanned for a fracture of the skull. He was in a *complete stupor* during the operation, and was not conscious of what took place. At fifteen he became seriously ill of fever. In the delirium occasioned by the fever, he gave a correct description of the operation, *and of all the persons present, their dress,* manners, and actions, to the minutest particulars. The "superior power" must have obtained this knowledge in some other way than through the ordinary channels of the outward senses.

In cases of apparent drowning, where the person has been saved from death by active, external help, we have been informed that the human mind has worked with a rapidity of action not thought possible in the waking state, the intensity of mental action being increased in adverse ratio to the inaction of the external senses and consciousness. In this state the career of a lifetime has been reviewed, conversations, actions, persons seen and places visited, all vividly brought to mind—in possibly less time than it takes to pen this paragraph. These phenomena suggest the reflection that the daily waking life—sensuous and worldly-minded—is possibly, to many, the least real and effective. How much our external life is influenced by our unconscious (to us in the waking state) sub-life, is an interesting problem?

Dr. Oliver Wendell Holmes says: "The more we examine the mechanism of thought, the more we shall see that the automatic and unconscious action of the mind enters largely into all its processes. We *all* have a *double* who is wiser and better than we, who puts thoughts into our heads and words into our mouths."

A commercial gentleman of my acquaintance, who was rather sceptical on the subject of double-consciousness—although, "notwithstanding," he said, "Mr. Stead, in the *Review of Reviews,* had turned an honest penny out of ghosts, double-consciousness, and that sort of rubbish"—admitted to me, he had a maid, who had an awkward habit of rising in her sleep, carefully setting the fires, cleaning and dusting out the rooms, setting the breakfast table, and doing many other things which appeared important to the servant-mind. Her movements were watched. She slipped about with eyes closed, avoiding obstacles, and doing her work systematically and neatly, and without fuss, when done, she would go to bed. In the morning she had no recollection of what she had said or done. It was a curious thing, he had to admit. The girl was honest enough. He was certain this habit had not been stimulated. Threats of discharge, and possible loss of wages, did not cure her of this habit. There was a certain form of "double consciousness" in this case.

"The subliminal consciousness" of Mr. Myers, by which he accounts for the phenomena of genius, is but another way of expressing the concept of an "identity underlying all consciousness," the psyche, the real "I, me," "the superior power which directs and controls our better nature," the "double who is wiser and better than we," the reality of which is so much hidden from our ordinary experience, because our soul-life is so much buried out of sight by the *débris* of the "things of this life," which, fortunately or otherwise, pre-occupy so much of our attention.

It is this "subliminal consciousness" we see manifested in the psychic state, and natural somnambulism. *Clairvoyance, Psychometry, Thought-Transference,* etc., are as so many spectrum rays of the one soul light. Call them "subliminal" if you will. These rays flow out from the soul, and are many-hued, distinct or blurred, according to the degree of pureness or super-sensitivity of the external corporeal prism through which they are projected.

Persons have lived for years, we are credibly informed, who have spent half their lives entranced, *in the alternation of two distinct individualities* or two distinct states of consciousness, in one of which they forget all they had learned or did in the other.

Professor Huxley described (*British Association of Science, Belfast, 1874*) a case in which two separate lives, a normal, and abnormal one, seemed to be lived at intervals by the same individual during the greater portion of her life.

The conclusion to the whole matter is—the psychic, or soul-powers in some persons are less entrammelled by the senses than in others; that a high degree of organic sensitiveness always accompanies those who are recognised as psychics or sensitives; that this state of sensitiveness is natural to some, and in others may be developed by accident, disease, or induced by *somnambulism and trance.*

I will endeavor to show these psychic characteristics, or soul gifts, underlie, and enter into the varied phenomena—*Clairvoyance, Psychometry, Thought-Transference, Thought-Reading,* and what not, which are collated under the title of, CLAIRVOYANCE AND THOUGHT-TRANSFERENCE.

CHAPTER II.

CLAIRVOYANCE.

What is *Clairvoyance?* The term *"Clairvoyance,"* is French, and means *clear-seeing,* but it appears to me to be an inadequate term, because it might signify clear optical vision, or clear *mental vision.* What is signified by the term is the power which certain individuals possess of seeing external objects under circumstances which render the sight of these objects impossible to physical optics. In short, by *Clairvoyance,* I mean the power which the *mind* has of seeing or knowing thoughts and psychical conditions, and objects hidden from or beyond the reach of the physical senses; and if the existence of this faculty can be established, we arrive at a demonstration that man has a power within his body as yet unrecognised by physical science—a power which is called soul, or mind-seeing, and for the description of such a power the term might be auto-nocticy or psychoscopy. Psychoscopy, or soul sight, would, perhaps, be the better term. I propose to use the old term—*Clairvoyance*—as it signifies, in popular usage, the power of seeing beyond the range of physical vision, as we know it.

That certain persons are endowed with this faculty of clear seeing—in some of its various phases—is a matter settled beyond dispute. What special name to call this faculty, or what are the true causes of its existence; why it should be possessed by some persons and not by others; why it should be so frail and fugitive in the presence of some people, and strong and vivid before others; *why some persons are never clairvoyant until they have been through the mesmeric and psychic states;* why some become possessed of the faculty through disease; while, with others, the gift of clairvoyance appears to be a spontaneous possession; and why some operators are successful in inducing *Clairvoyance,* and others not, etc., are interesting questions to which the student of psychology may, with advantage, direct his attention.

Clairvoyance is soul-sight—the power of the soul to see. It is the state of refined psychic perception. This state increases in lucidity—clearness and power of penetration—in proportion as the activity of the physical senses is reduced below normal action. It is observed to be most effective in the trance state—natural or induced—as in the mesmeric and psychic states. I conclude, then, clairvoyance depends upon the unfolding of the spirit's perception, and is increased in power as the ascendency of the spirit arises above the activities of the spirit's corporeal envelope—the body. In proportion to the spirit's ascendency over the organs and senses of the body, is this psychic gift perfect or imperfect.

The large brain or cerebrum is the physical organ of the soul as the cerebellum is of the physiological brain functions. Mental functions are manifested by the former, and physical functions by the latter. .

Clairvoyance, as a spiritual faculty, will doubtless have its appropriate organ in the brain. I do not profess to locate that organ. At the same time I have noticed the best clairvoyants are wide and full between the eyes, showing there is a particular fulness of the frontal cerebral lobes, at their juncture at the root of the nose. This may be something more than a mere physiognomic sign. When this sign is accompanied by refinement of organisation, and a fine type of brain, I always look for the possible manifestation of *Clairvoyance* in mesmeric subjects.

Some writers are of the opinion *Clairvoyance* is actually soul-sight, more or less retarded in lucidity by the action or activity of the body senses. Others believe it to be a state arising from a peculiar highly-strained nervous condition, which induces the state of super-sensitivity or impressionability of the organisation. The first may be termed the spiritual, and the latter the physiological hypothesis. But, as a matter of fact, both conditions are noted. The latter may account for much, and possibly is sufficient to explain much that is called thought-reading—so often mistaken for clairvoyance. It does appear to me that certain peculiar physiological conditions, varying from semi-consciousness to profound trance, are necessary for the manifestation of clairvoyance, even when it takes place in apparently normal life of the possessor.

The ornate and mystic ceremonies indulged in by *Hindu mystics, Egyptian, Grecian,* and *Roman* priests, have the one grand end in view—viz., to induce the requisite state of super-sensitivity, and thus prepare the consecrated youths, sybils, and vestal virgins for the influx of spiritual vision, prophecy, and what not. When this subtle influx came—by whatever name called —the phenomena manifested were pretty much the same as we know them, only varied in degree. The gods spoke per oracle, *Pythean,* or *Delphic.* The man of God either coronated a king or foretold the end of a dynasty. St. Stephen saw *Christ,* St. John beheld visions, *Joan of Arc* was directed, *Swedenborg* illuminated, and religious ecstatics in ancient and modern times partook more or less of the sacred fire—the inner sight. This (stripped of the fantastic surroundings, priestly mummeries, and dominant belief of the times) simply indicated the evolution and exercise of clairvoyance and other psychic gifts.

Coming nearer home, we hear of the mysterious visions at the *Knock,* and at *Lourdes.* Miraculous appearances of the *Virgin* and winged angels, to cheer the hearts of the faithful, and to cause the heads of the scornful to rejoice in sceptical derision. Then we have all the vagaries produced by the high nervous tension of modern revivalisms, in which the visions seen are but a transformation of church and chapel dogmas into objective realities. These illusionary visions—mistaken for *Clairvoyance*—possess less reality than the delusive fancies of the sensitive in the state of hypnosis.

Clairvoyance will be governed by its own spiritual laws, just as sight is affected or retarded by physical conditions. What these spiritual laws are many can only surmise, but this they may safely conjecture—viz., that soul-sight is not trammelled or limited by the natural laws which govern physical optics. Clairvoyance and physical vision are absolutely distinct, and possess little in common.

To illustrate a new subject, it is permissible to draw upon the old and the well-known. So I venture to illustrate clairvoyance by certain facts in connection with ordinary human vision. Although some children see better than others, the power to see, with the ability to understand the relative positions and uses of the things seen, is a matter of development. In psychic vision, we also see growth or development, with increasing power to use and understand the faculty. Some children are blind from birth, and others, seeing, lose the power of sight. Many are *blind,* although they have physical sight, they see not with *the educated eye.* Many, again, have greater powers of sight than they are aware of. And so it is with psychic vision.

What is true of the physical is also true of the psychic. From the first glimmerings, to the possession of well-defined sight, a period of growth and time elapses. From the first incoherent cry of infancy to

well defined and intelligent speech of manhood, we
notice the same agencies at work. Not only is *Clairvoyant* vision generally imperfect at first, but the psychic's powers of description are also at fault. St. Paul
could not give utterance to what he saw, when caught
up to the third heavens. His knowledge of things and
powers of speech failed him to describe the startling,
the new, and the unutterable. He had a sudden revela-
tion of the state of things in a sphere which had no
counterparts in his previous experience, in this—his
known—world. Hence, although he knew of his
change of state, he could give no lawful or intelligible
expression to his thoughts.

Between the first incongruous utterances, and apparent fantastic blunderings, and the more mature
period in which *"things spiritual"* can be suitably described in our language, to our right sense of things,
or comprehension, a period of development and education must elapse. It is true some clairvoyants develop much more readily than others.

In the *entrancement* of the *Mesmeric* and *Psychic*
states, there is a lack of external consciousness. The
soul is so far liberated from the body as to act independently of the ordinary sensuous conditions of the
body, and sees by the perception and light of the inner
or spiritual world, as distinct from the perception and
light of this external or physical world. Elevated, or
rather, liberated into this new condition, the clairvoyant loses connection with the thrums and threads of
the physical organism, and is unable, or forgets for a
time, how to speak of things as they are, or as they
would appear to the physical vision of another. It is
not surprising that in the earlier stages of *Clairvoyant*
development, and consequent transfer of ordinary consciousness and sensuous perception to that of spiritual
consciousness and perception, the language of the *Clairvoyant* should appear peculiar, incongruous, and "want-

ing" according to our ideas of clearness and precision.

One important lesson may be learned from this— viz., *the operator should never force results, or strive to develop psychic perception by short cuts.* Time must be allowed to the sensitive, for training and experience, and the development of self-confidence and expression.

Clairvoyance is not a common possession. Nevertheless, I believe there any many persons who possess the faculty unknown to themselves. By following out patiently, for a time, the requisite directions, the possession of this invaluable psychic gift might be discovered by many who now appear totally devoid of any *Clairvoyant* indications. Its cultivation is possible and, in many ways, desirable.

"The higher attainment of *Occult* knowledge and power, the development of intuition, the psychometric senses, *Clairvoyant Vision,* inner hearing, etc., etc., thus reached, so open the avenues to a higher education, and enlarge the boundaries of human consciousness and activity, as to fairly dwarf into insignificance the achievements of external science."

Clairvoyance is as old as mankind, but the exhibition of *Clairvoyance,* induced by mesmeric processes, was first announced, outside of *India* by Puysegeur, a favorite pupil of Mesmer, in 1784. Since that time to the present day not only have remarkable cases of clairvoyance cropped up, in Europe and America, but there have been few mesmerists of any experience who have not had numerous cases under observation. *Clairvoyance* converted Dr. John Elliotson, F. R. S., one of the most scientific of British physicians, from extreme materialistic views to that of belief in soul and immortality. The same may be said of the late Dr. Ashburner, who was one of the Queen's physicians. Dr. Georget, author of *"Physiology of the Nervous System,"*—who was at one time opposed to a belief in the existence of a transcendental state in man,—found

upon examination of the facts and incidents of artificial somnambulism, that *his materialism must go.* In
his last will and testament, referring to the above-men-
tioned works, he says: "This work had scarcely appeared, when renewed meditations on a very extraordinary phenomenon, somnambulism, no longer per-
mitted me to entertain doubts of the existence within
us, and external to us, of an intelligent principle, altogether different from material existences; in a word,
of the soul of God. With respect to this I have a profound conviction, founded upon facts which I believe
to be incontestable." *"Dr. Georget directed this
change of opinion should have full publicity after his
death.*

Space would not suffice me to mention the names of
all the highly educated and refined minds, in the medical, literary, philosophic, and scientific walks of life,
who have studied these phenomena, and who, like Dr.
Georget, have no more doubts of their reality than
they have of their own physical existence, status, or
reputation. Among medical men—some of whom I
have known and corresponded with—might be mentioned *Sir James Simpson, Drs. Elliotson, Ashburner,
Esdaile, Buss, Garth Wilkinson, Hands, Wyld, Hitch-
man, Eadon, and Davey.* Among others on the roll
of fame, might be noticed *Archbishop Whately, Earls
Ducie, Stanhope, Macclesfield, Charville;* the present
*Duke of Argyle; Lord R. Cavendish, Lord Lindsay;
Burton,* the traveller; and the late *Sergeant Cox.*
Among literary men, *Mr. Gladstone,* Britain's fore-
most statesman and scholar; *Mr. Balfour,* his able and
talented opponent; *Bulwer Lytton, Marryat, Neal,
Robert Chambers, Dickens,* and *Stevenson,* of *"Dr.
Jekyll* and *Mr. Hyde"* fame. *Mr. George Combe,*
the distinguished Scottish metaphysician, philosopher,
author, phrenologist, etc., was profoundly interested
in the phenomena. Among well-known men of science

might be mentioned *Camillie Flammarion*, the French astronomer; *Fichte*, the German philosopher; *Professors Tornebom* and *Edland*, Swedish physicists; *Professor Oliver Lodge, D.Sc., F.R.S.; Alfred Russell Wallace, D.C.L., LL.D.; William Crookes, F.R.S.; Cromwell F. Varley, F.R.S.* Notwithstanding this somewhat formidable array of investigators of *Clairvoyance*, many good people will not hesitate to deny the value of such evidence, and yet will believe anything in its favor which may be found in the Bible, as to its existence in the *past*. It is a strange perversion of judgment—not at all surprising—when the majority take (second-hand) for their religious (?) views whatever is recognised as "sound" in each particular district and Church. *It is not a question of belief, it is a "question of evidence," as Mr. Gladstone avers.*

The *Rev. Mr. M'Kinnon*, late pastor of *Chalmers' Free Church, Glasgow*, told me a short time ago, "*Clairvoyance* was nothing more than a high nervous concentrated form of mental vision," to which I replied, "*Admitting the hypothesis—which, however, explained nothing—it matters little what Clairvoyance is esteemed to be or called, if the facts connected with it are acknowledged.*" Even this friend admitted he knew a man in Mull, who lived on the half croft, next to his father's croft. This man had great repute in that district as "*having the Second Sight.*" Whatever this man foretold always came to pass. One instance will suffice. He (Mr. M'Kinnon) remembered that one day, while this crofter (who was a tailor by trade) was working, he suddenly stopped, and looked *out into vacancy*—as he always did when the "Second Sight was on him"—and described a funeral coming over the hill, the mourners, who they were and numbers, the way the procession took, and the name of the "man whose face was covered," and finally, when the procession would appear. Mr. M'Kinnon's parents noted the time, and being simple Highland folk, accustomed to the accuracy of this man's visions, they believed what he said, and kept his saying in their hearts till the time of fulfillment came about. Mr. M'Kinnon assured me "the funeral took place to the day and hour, twelve months subsequently to the vision, as predicted." *All I can say is, if "a high nervous concentrated form of mental vision" is capable of pointing out all this, it is worthy of investigation.* It is evident this tailor at least had a power of vision—prevoyance—not of the ordinary, everyday kind of vision. *Second sight, as exhibited in this case, is what may be termed spontaneous clairvoyance.*

Epes Sargent, in his work, *"The Scientific Basis of Spiritualism,"* referring to *Clairvoyance,* says: "As far as I have admitted it as part of a scientific basis (demonstrating man's spiritual nature), it is the exercise of the supersensual faculty of penetrating opaque and dense matter as if by the faculty of sight. But it does more. It detects our unuttered, undeveloped thoughts; it goes back along the past, and describes what is hidden; nay, the proofs are overwhelming that it may pierce the future, and predict coming events from the shadows they cast before.

"What is it that sees without the physical eyes, and without the assistance of light? What is normal sight? It is not the vibrating ether—it is not the external eye —that sees. It is the soul using the eye as an instrument, and light as a condition. Prove once that sight can exist without the use of light, sensation, or any physical organ of vision, and you prove an abnormal, supersensual, spiritual faculty—a proof which puts an end to the theory of materialism, and which, through its affinity with analogous or corresponding facts, justifies its introduction as part of a scientific basis for the spiritual theory."

J. F. Deleuze was profoundly convinced of the existence of this faculty. He claimed that the power of seeing at a distance, prevision, and the transference of thought without the aid of external signs, were in themselves sufficient proofs of the existence of spirituality of soul.

Except in a very few instances, little or no pains are taken to cultivate the spiritual nature of man. *Civilised man of to-day is but rising out of the age of brute force of yesterday, and he is still circumscribed by love of earthly power and position. He is an acquisitive rather than a spiritual being.* Being dominated by the senses, he will naturally seek and appreciate that which gratifies his senses most. He has little time or patience for anything which does not contribute pleasure to his sensuous nature. He would give time to the investigation of the soul side of life if it brought gold, the means of enjoyment, and gratified his acquisitiveness and love of power. Probably the majority give the subject no attention at all. If the spiritual side of men's natures were as fully cultivated as those elements which bring them bread and butter and praise in the market-place, there is no doubt, no manner of doubt whatever, but the most of them would occupy a nobler and more spiritually elevated plane in life; and were adequate means taken, I doubt not but this faculty of clairvoyance would become more generally known and cultivated. Even to the selfish, worldly, and non-spiritual man, *Clairvoyance* is not without its practical side and utility, such, for instance, as supplying Chicago with water. To the spiritually minded, *Clairvoyance* and all psychic gifts are appreciated, less for what they will bring, than for the testimony they present of man's spiritual origin, transcendental powers and probable continuity of life beyond this mortal vale.

CHAPTER III.

CLAIRVOYANCE ILLUSTRATED.

Clairvoyance may be briefly classified as, FAR and
NEAR, DIRECT and INDIRECT, OBJECTIVE and SUB-
JECTIVE. I propose to give a few well-authenticated
cases to illustrate these phases in this CHAPTER.

FAR AND DIRECT CLAIRVOYANCE.

This is possibly the highest and purest combination.
The sensitive is able to state facts not within the range
of the knowledge of those present. Thus when *Swedenborg* discribed to the *Queen* and her friends, when
at a distance of several hundred miles from the con-
flagration, the burning of her palace at *Christiania,*
no one present could possibly know of the fire or the
incidents connected therewith. Hence no thought-
reading, brain-picking, much less guess-work or coincidence, could account for the exactness of details
given by the seer. *Clairvoyance in this case was not
only far and direct, but objective.* That is, the matter
recorded was connected with the physical or objective plane.

CLAIRVOYANCE AN AID TO SCIENCE.

Chicago, Ill., as is well known, is one of the most
go-ahead cities in the world. Like *Jonah's* gourd it
appeared to spring up in a night. Its population
rapidly increased, and water soon became a *sine qua
non,* both as regards use and luxury. Science was at

fault; for geologists had pronounced that there could be no water beneath such strata. Top water was all that could be looked for, and presently a water company was formed to supply this impure kind of liquid.

"There happened to live at this time in Chicago a person named *Abraham James,* a simple-minded man, of *Quaker* descent, uneducated, and in fact, quite an ignorant person. It was discovered by a Mrs. Caroline Jordon that James was a natural clairvoyant, in fact a medium, and that he had declared when put into the trance condition that both water and petroleum, in large quantities, would be found in a certain tract of land in the neighboorhood of the city. For a long time no attention was paid to his statements. At length two gentlemen from Maine, called Whitehead and Scott, coming to Chicago on business, and hearing what had been said by Abraham James, had him taken to the land where he said water could be had in immense quantities by boring for. Being entranced, James at once pointed out the very spot. He told them that he not only saw the water, but could trace its source from the Rocky Mountains, 2,000 miles away, to the spot on which they stood, and could sketch out on maps the strata and caverns through which it ran. Negotiations were at once entered into for the purchase of the land, and the work of boring was commenced. This was in Ferbuary, 1864, and the process went on daily till November, when, having reached a depth of 711 feet, water was struck, and flowed up at once at the rate of 600,000 gallons every 24 hours.

"The borings showed the following kinds of strata passed through by the drill, and this was spiritually seen and described by the *Clairvoyant* as practical proofs to the senses of other people. First the drill passed through alluvium soil, 100 feet; limestone, saturated with oil, 35 feet, which would burn as well as any coal; Joliet marble, 100 feet; *conglomerate strata* of sand and flint, mixed with iron pyrites and traces of copper, 125 feet; rock (shale) saturated with petroleum, the sediment coming up like putty, thick and greasy, 156 feet; galena limestone was next reached at a depth of 530 feet; a bed of limestone, containing flint and sulphuret of iron was bored through, the depth being 639 feet, and being very hard, the work went on slowly. At this point there appeared a constant commotion arising from the escape of gas, the water suddenly falling from 30 to 60 feet, and then as suddenly rising to the surface, carrying with it chippings from the drill, and other matters. The work still went on; when at the depth of 711 feet the arch on the rock was penetrated, and the water suddenly burst forth from a bore 4½ inches at the bottom, of a temperature of 58° F., clear as crystal, pure as diamond, and perfectly free from every kind of animal and vegetable matter, and which, for drinking purposes and health, is much better adapted than any water yet known, and will turn out to be the poor man's friend for all time to come.

"Here, then, is a huge fact for the faithless; the fact brought to light by dynamite or invisible agency, and which no power of negation can gainsay. Natural science said, No water could be found; but psychology said—False, for I will point out the spot where it will flow in splendid streams as long as the earth spins on its axis. Since 1864 the artesian well of Chicago has poured forth water at the rate of a million and a half gallons daily; and what is economic, to say nothing of Yankee shrewdness, it is conveyed into ponds or reservoirs which in winter freeze, producing 40,-000 tons of ice for sale, and which might be quadrupled at any time. "*

---

* "Phrenological Annual," 1892. Extract from article by Dr. Samuel Eadon, M.D., M.A., LL.D. and Ph.D., etc., Aberdeen and Edinburgh Universities. ,

This is a case of far and near, direct and objective Clairvoyance. This historical incident proves the value and reality of psychic vision.

Indirect Clairvoyance is the power of discerning what may be more or less in the minds of those present, including absent or forgotten thoughts and incidents. Thus, when a clairvoyant discribes a place with accuracy, recognised by some one present to be correct, and also gives details partly known and unknown, but afterwards found to be correct, this mixture of phases may be recognised as indirect.

SUBJECTIVE CLAIRVOYANCE.

Subjective Clairvoyance is that phase which enables the sensitive to perceive things and ideas on the spiritual or subjective plane. The late *Rev. Stainton Moses,* well known in literary circles as *"M.A., Oxon,"* once asked the following pertinent questions: "Is there conceivably a mass of life all round us of which most of us have no cognisance? One gifted lady I know sees *clairvoyantly* the spirit-life of all organised things, of a tree or plant for example. I have heard her describe what her interior faculties perceive. Is it a fact that spirit, underlying everything, can be so perceived by the awakened faculties?" I should say yes. If this lady's clairvoyance has been of a high order in other respects—why not in this? *This type of psychic vision is of the subjective order.*

There are necessarily an infinite variety of phases, pure and mixed, which the investigator will meet in practice. These phases may be called *far,* such as seeing objects, etc., at a distance—prevoyance, predicting events; retrovoyance, reading the past; introvoyance, seeing internally, or examining bodies, as in disease; external introvoyance, seeing into lockets, packets, letters, safes, and discovering hidden, known or forgotten, or lost objects. Lastly, there is pseudo-clairvoyance. For one case of direct there are hundreds of well authenticated cases of indirect clairvoyance, and again for one of the latter there are thousands of pseudo-clairvoyance, which are the outcome of states similar to hypnosis, and are nothing more than an incongruous medley of suggested ideas and fancies. Thus a strong and positive willed person can impinge his ideas through the thought-atmosphere of the sensitive and distort or deflect the psychic vision, and render abortive any attempts to get beyond the circle of the dominating influence. Again, the sensitive may enter a realm of fancy—a veritable dreamland of coherent and incoherent ideation, either the product of the sensitive's own condition, or of suggestion—accidental, spontaneous, and determined—in the sensitive's surroundings. Of course any classification of the numerous phases of *Clairvoyance* must be purely arbitrary.

DIRECT AND OBJECTIVE CLAIRVOYANCE—LOST GOODS RESTORED.

This instance of far vision is taken from *"A Tangled Yarn," page 173, "Leaves from Captain James Payn's Log,"* which was published recently by C. H. Kelly. As I knew Captain Hudson, of Swansea, personally, and heard from his own lips the following incident, I have much pleasure in introducing it here as a further illustration of the *Cui bono* of *Clairvoyance:*—

"The *Theodore* got into Liverpool the same day as the *Bland*. She was a larger ship than ours but had a similar cargo. The day that I went to the owners to report 'all right,' I met with Captain Morton in a terrible stew because he was thirty bales of cotton short, a loss equal to the whole of his own wages and

the mate's into the bargain.   He was so fretted over
it that his wife in desperation recommended him to
get the advice of a Captain Hudson, who had a young
female friend clever as a *Clairvoyant*.   We were both
sceptical in the matter of clairvoyance.   At first Morton didn't wish to meddle, he said, with 'a parcel of
modern witchcraft,' and that sort of thing; but he
at last yielded to his wife's urgency and consented
to go.   There was first of all a half-crown fee to
Captain Hudson, and then the way was clear for an
interview with the young clairvoyant.   I was present
to 'see fair.'   When the girl had been put into the
clairvoyant state Morton was instructed to take her
right hand in his right hand and ask her any questions
he wished.   The replies were in substance as follows :—
*She went back mentally to the port whence the Theo-
dore had sailed, retracing with her hand as she in
words also described the course of the ship from Liverpool across the Atlantic, through the West Indian
group, etc., back to New Orleans.*   At length she said,
'Yes, this is the place where the cotton is lost; it's
put on board a big black ship with a red mark round
it.'   Then she began to trace with her hand and describe the homeward course of the vessel, but after
re-crossing the Atlantic, instead of coming up the *Irish
Channel* for *Liverpool,* she turned along the *English
Channel* as though bound for the coast of *France;* and
then stretching out her hand she exclaimed, 'Oh, here's
the cotton; but what funny people they are; they
don't talk English.'   Captain Morton said at once, 'I
see; it's the *Brunswick,* Captain Thomas,' an American ship that lay alongside of him at New Orleans
and was taking in her cargo of cotton while the *Theodore* was loading, and was bound for *Havre de Grace.*
Captain Morton, satisfied with his *Clairvoyant's* information, went home and wrote immediately to Captain Thomas, inquiring for his lost cargo.   In due

course he got an answer that the cotton was certainly there, that it had been taken off the wharf in mistake, and that it was about to be sold for whomsoever it might concern; but that if he (Captain Morton) would remit a certain amount to cover freight and expenses, the bales should be forwarded to him at once. He did so, and in due time received the cotton, subject only to the expenses of transit from Havre to Liverpool." *Such are the facts; I do not offer any explanation, for none are needed.*

CLAIRVOYANCE AN AID TO THE PHYSICIAN.

I am indebted to Dr. George Wyld for this case, which also exhibits the value of *Clairvoyance.* Dr. Wyld had the good fortune to make the acquaintance of a Mrs. D——, a lady in private life who was endowed with the gift of natural *Clairvoyance.* Dr. Wyld told his lady of "a friend who had for years suffered intense agony for hours every night in his back and chest, and that latterly he had been obliged to sit up all night in a chair, and his legs began to swell."

"This gentleman had regularly for three years been under many of the leading physicians of London. Some said that there must be some obscure heart affection, others said it was neuralgia, one said it was gout, and the last consulted said it was malignant caries of the spine."

Dr. Wyld's friend called upon him by appointment, and met Mrs. D——. This lady merely looked at him. When he had retired from the room Mrs. D—— made the following statement of his case to the doctor:—
"I have seen what the disease is; I saw it as distinctly as if the body were transparent. There is a tumour behind the heart, about the size of a walnut; it is of a dirty colour; and it jumps and looks as if it would

burst. Nothing can do him any good but entire rest."

"I at once saw," says Dr. Wyld, "what she meant, and sat down to write to my friend's medical attendant as follows:—

"I believe I have discovered the nature of Mr. ——'s disease. He has an aneurism on the descending *aorta*, about the size of a walnut. It is this which causes the slight displacement which has been observed in the heart, and the pressure of the tumour against the intercostal nerves is the cause of the agony in the back, and the peripheral pains in the front of the chest. You are going to-morrow to see Sir —— in consulation; show him this diagnosis, and let me know what he says."

"Next, the patient had the consultation, and Mrs. D——'s diagnosis was confirmed; and the doctors agreed with Mrs. D—— the only thing to be done was to take entire rest. The treatment was duly followed up, with successful results." Dr. Wyld thoughtfully adds—"It is true that the diagnosis cannot be absolutely confirmed during life, but as the profession unanimously pronounce the disease to be aneurism, the diagnosis may be accepted as correct. This diagnosis has probably saved the gentleman's life, as before Mrs. D—— saw him he was allowed to shoot over Scotch moors, and to ride, drive, and play billiards."

The use of *Clairvoyance* in the diagnosis of disease is by no means as rare as the majority of physicians and the general public would naturally assume. I have had many opportunities of witnessing the accuracy of diagnosis and the excellence of the methods of treatment advised by *Clairvoyants*. In my own personal experience I have had much evidence of correctness of *Clairvoyance* in diagnosis, and subsequent success in treatment. It is a phase most desirable to cultivate if possible, and all allied conditions connected therewith.

TRAVELLING CLAIRVOYANCE.

As a public entertainer at one time, giving demonstrations of mesmeric phenomena, I have had naturally many opportunities of seeing different types of *Clairvoyance*. During a course of entertainments given by me in Rothesay, 1881, I was able to introduce *Clairvoyance* to public notice by the most difficult method, that of public experiments.

M. C., the *Clairvoyante*, was a native of *Newcastle-on-Tyne*. All her clairvoyant experiments were satisfactory. Her husband was also a *Clairvoyant*, but not so striking for public exhibition. M. C. seemed to possess all phases. One or two experiments out of many will be interesting not only as illustrative of *Clairvoyance*, but because what I relate can be easily ratified.

M. C. arrived in Rothesay for the first time about four hours previously to taking her seat upon the platform, in the New Public Halls. It was neither possible nor probable she could have obtained the information she possessed by other than psychic means. The clairvoyant was mesmerised and blindfolded before the audience. After some experiments in objective clairvoyance were given, such as describing a watch, telling the time, and the number, by having the watch held silently over her forehead, she gave several experiments in travelling clairvoyance. Many visitors in the hall—for Rothesay is a well known and fashionable seaside resort—sent up requests to the platform, and desired the *Clairvoyante* should visit their homes in Kent, Cornwall, Island of Jersey, in the Isle of Man, Glasgow, and other places. Her visits and descriptions were in all instances extremely satisfactory. How far thought-transference and objective clairvoyance commingled and entered into her descriptions it would be difficult to say, but the results were simply marvellous.

Test case, by the late Dr. Maddever, M.D., M.R. C.S., and Dr. John Maddever, his son. These medical gentlemen resided in Rothesay, and were present in the hall. Dr. Maddever desired me to send the clairvoyante into a certain room in his house and that she should describe it.

All the directions the *Clairvoyante* obtained were, "to go out of the hall, down the front steps; when out turn to the right and proceed onward till she came to an iron-railed gate, on which was a small brass plate, bearing the name of 'Dr. Maddever,' she was to open the gate, go up to the hall-door, enter, pass the first door to the left, and turn round a passage to the left and enter the first door to which she came, and describe what she saw."

Sitting still upon the platform in silence for a minute or two, she suddenly exclaimed:—*"I am at the gate—at the door—now in the hall—I have found the room, and I am now inside, and stand with my back to the door."* She then proceeded to describe the room, the book-cases which surrounded it, their peculiar structure; the mantel-piece, the form of the clock, the time, and the appearance of the ornaments. The table in the centre of the room, its form, the color and style of the cloth upon it, books, albums, and papers thereon, the flower vase support in the window, and a number of other particulars.

At the conclusion Dr. Maddever arose in the audience and said:—*Ladies and gentlemen, Dr. de Laurence is a stranger to me, I only know of him by report. The young lady on the platform I do not know. I have not seen either till this evening, and they have never been in my house. The experiment we have had is most remarkable, and should be of deep and profound interest to all. The young lady has de-*

scribed the room, as far as I can remember, most correctly—in fact very much better than I could have done myself." This statement was received with applause. After one or two instances of travelling *Clairvoyance,* a young gentleman rose in the body of the hall and desired I should send the sensitive to a house or villa not far from the juncture of Marine Place and Ardbeg Road.

The directions given to the *Clairvoyante* were briefly to the effect, she was to leave the place, on reaching the front street she was to turn to her left and keep on past the Post Office, Esplanade, past the Skeoch Woods, etc., till she came to the house. She nodded her head in compliance, and presently announced she "had found the house." Then she shivered and appeared to draw back, and said *"I won't go in."*

Some persons in the audience laughed, and one (I think it was the young gentleman who asked that she might be sent) said: "The whole thing is a swindle." Now, considering there was not a single flaw in the experiments that night, surprise after surprise being given, and the audience had risen in enthusiasm, this opinion was not favorably received.

I asked the gentleman "to have patience." I had no doubt but we would know soon enough the reasons. "Whatever they were I would try and ascertain them."

With much hesitancy she declared that "the house was not one any respectable female would enter, and she would not." When I repeated this statement to the audience, there was what the newspapers call "sensation." The sensation was intensified when one of the Rothesay Magistrates, Bailie Molloy, the then senior Bailie of the Royal Burgh, declared *"the young woman was right, perfectly right, this was a house which had been inadvertently let to persons of ill-fame, and he, for one, had recently had the facts of the case placed before him, and he was most anxious that these people should be put out, and they would be, as soon as the proper steps could be taken."*

The young gentleman retired somewhat discomfited, and the excitement produced by these and other experiments brought crowded houses during my professional stay in England.

When my *"mesmeric exposition"* was concluded, the two medical gentlemen referred to, were good enough to introduce themselves, and invited me to call next day to see the room. I accepted the invitation during the following day and saw how truly correct and vivid her description had been. In the first experiment the sensitive described the state of the doctor's library, pointing out what had not been recollected by either of the medical men, and I believe the other case comes under the heading of direct and objective clairvoyance. Dr. Maddever's house was about a quarter of a mile, and the other house about a mile and a half from the hall.

The persistent and reliable *Clairvoyance* evinced by this sensitive was induced. *She was a mesmeric subject, and when such subjects are properly treated they make the very best Clairvoyants.*

Psychic Vision Possessed By The Blind.

Mrs. Croad resided at Redland, Bristol. My attention was called to her case some years ago by Dr. J. G. Davey, of Bristol. Unfortunately circumstances at the time prevented a personal visit and report. Her psychic gifts and wonderful supersensitivity have been amply testified to, by most reliable witnesses, such as Dr. Davey, Hy. G. Atkinson, F.G.S., and others.

Clairvoyance in Mrs. Croad's case was and is (for I believe the lady is still living) a singular admixture of subtle sense transference so well known to mesmerists of the old school, and spontaneous psychic vision. *Thought-transference* and indirect *Clairvoy-*

ance, more or less induced, by intence voluntary concentration.

Mrs. Croad is deaf, dumb, and paralysed, and stone blind. She can see and hear, read with powers "denied to ordinary mortals," and discern pictures and writings in the dark. She is aware of her daughter's thoughts when the latter touches her, and becomes at once acquainted with what her daughter wishes to communicate. She possesses supersensitivity of touch, and discerns colour by their degrees of heat, roughness or smoothness. She can also identify photographs and pictures in the same way. From time to time she has exhibited the highest phases of *Clairvoyance.* Reports have been made in this case by medical experts in the *Journal of Psychological Medicine,* and other magazines and journals several years ago. The most recent was contributed by the Rev. Taliesin Dans, The Cottage, Claptons, to *The Review of Reviews* in January, 1891.

THE SPIRITUALISTIC AND PRACTICAL CHARACTER OF CLAIRVOYANCE

might be further illustrated by the well-known case of Miss Eliza Hamilton, who became paralysed in her limbs and right arm, through severe injury to the spine. She had been in hospital for four months, on her return home frequently passed into the trance state, and on awakening described various people and places she had visited, and objects seen. These descriptions have been invariably verified subsequently. "She also at times," says her physician, "speaks of having been in the company of persons with whom she was acquainted in this world, but who have passed away; and she tells her friends that they have become more beautiful, and have cut off their infirmities with which they were afflicted while here. She often describes events which *are about to happen,* and these are always fulfilled exactly as she predicts.

"Her father," says Mr. Hudson Tuttle, "read in her presence a letter he had received from a friend in Leeds, speaking of the loss of his daughter, about whose fate he was very unhappy, as she had disappeared nearly a month before, and left no trace. Eliza went into the trance state, and cried out, 'Rejoice! I have found the lost girl! She is happy in the angel world.' She said the girl had fallen into the dark water where dyers washed their cloths; that her friends could not have found her had they sought her there, *but* now the body had floated a few miles, and would be found in the River Aire. The body was found as described.

"Now, knowing that her eyes were closed, that she could not hear, that her bodily senses were in profound lethargy, how are we to account for the intensity and keenness of sight? Her mental powers were exceedingly exalted, and scarcely a question could be asked her but she correctly answered.

"In this case the independence of the mind of the physical body is shown in every instance of *Clairvoyance,* is proven beyond cavil or doubt. If it is demonstrated that the mind sees without the aid of eyes, hears when the ears are deaf, feels when the nerves of sensation are at rest, it follows that it is independent of these outward avenues, and has other channels of communication with the external world essentially its own."

CLAIRVOYANCE FROM DISEASE

Miss Mollie Fancher, of Brooklyn Heights, fell off a tramway car when eighteen years of age, experienced very severe injuries to head and spine, her body being dragged a distance, through her dress catching on

the step of the car. She became paralysed, lost all
her senses, except touch. She gradually recovered
hearing, taste, and ability to talk in time. She was
also blind for nine years. Drs. Speir and Ormiston
were her physicians, men of skill and marked probity.
These, with a veritable host of medical men—ministers
of the Gospel, educationists, and specialists—have
borne testimony to her remarkable endowments, from
which we take two extracts. Mr. Charles Ewart, Prin-
cipal of the Brooklyn Heights Seminary, where she
was under special care, writes :—

"For many days together she has been to all appearances dead. The slightest pulse could not be detected;
there was no evidence of respiration. Her limbs were
as cold as ice, and had there not been some warmth
about her heart, she would have been buried. When
I first saw her she had but one sense—that of touch.
By running her fingers over the printed page, she could
read with equal facility in light or darkness. The
most delicate work is done by her in the night. . . . .
Her power of clairvoyance, or second sight, is mar-
vellously developed. *Distance imposes no barriers,*
without the slightest error she dictates the contents
of sealed letters which have never been in her hands.
She discriminates in darkness the most delicate shades
of colour. She writes with extraordinary rapidity."

*Mr. Henry M. Parkhurst, the astronomer (residing
at 173 Gates Avenue, Brooklyn, N. Y.), writes:—*

"From the waste-basket of a New York gentleman
acquaintance he fished an unimportant business letter,
without reading it, tore it into ribbons, and tore the
ribbons into squares. He shook the pieces well together, put them into an envelope, and sealed it. This
he subsequently handed to Miss Fancher. The blind
girl took the envelope in her hand, and passed her hand
over it several times, called for paper and pencil, and

wrote it verbatim   The seal of the letter had not been broken.   Mr. Parkhurst himself opened it, pasted the contents together, and compared the two.   Miss Fancher's was a literal copy of the original."

MESMERIC CLAIRVOYANCE AND SPIRITUALISM.

"A few evenings ago I called upon Mr. and Mrs. Loomis, 2 Vernon Place, Bloomsbury, and after we had chatted for a short time in the drawing-room with the door closed and nobody else present, I asked if they would try a mesmeric experiment for me.   They willingly agreed, and Mr. Loomis, by passes, threw his wife into a mesmeric state, as he often does, and an intelligence, which claimed to be the spirit of her mother, spoke through her lips.   Until this moment I had said nothing to any living soul about the nature of my contemplated experiment, but I then asked the unseen intelligence if it could then and there go to the house of Mrs. Macdougall Gregory, 21 Green Street, Grosvenor Square, London, and move a heavy physical object in her presence.   The reply was, I do not know, I will try.   About three minutes afterwards, at 8.40 p.m., the intelligence said that Mrs. Gregory was in her drawing-room with a friend, and added, 'I have made Mrs. Gregory feel a prickly sensation in her arm from the elbow down to the hand, as if some person had squeezed the arm, and she has spoken about it to her friend.'

"I took a note in writing of this statement at the time it was made.   A few minutes later I left Mr. and Mrs. Loomis, and without telling them my intention to do so, went straight to the house of Mrs. Gregory about a mile and a half off.   I had selected Mrs. Gregory for this experiment because she is not afraid to publish her name in connection with psychic truths, and her word carries weight, especially in Scotland, where she and her family are well-known. She is the widow of Professor Gregory, of Edinburgh University, and is a lineal descendant of the Lord of the Isles. I then for the first time told Mrs. Gregory of the experiment. She replied that between half-past eight and nine o'clock that evening she was playing the piano, and suddenly turned round to her friend, Miss Yauewicz, of Upper Norwood, saying, 'I don't know what is the matter with me, I feel quite stupid, and have such a pain in my right arm that I cannot go on playing.' Miss Yauewicz, who was no believer in spiritualism or any of the marvels of psychology, felt a lively interest when she was informed of the experiment. She told me that she clearly remembered Mrs. Gregory's statement that she could not go on playing because of the pain in her right arm." *

Mrs. Loomis was a remarkable *Clairvoyante*, whom I accidentally became acquainted with in Liverpool many years ago, shortly after her arrival from America. I introduced the lady and her husband, Mr. Daniel Loomis, to Mr. Harris, then editor of *The Spiritualist*. The Guion steamer, *Idaho*, in which they came from New York, was wrecked off the Irish Coast, and all they possessed in this world was lost with the vessel. Mrs. Loomis predicted the disaster, where it was likely to take place; that all hands would be saved, but all they had lost. Upon the arrival of the officers of the vessel in Liverpool, they presented Mrs. Loomis, at the Bee Hotel, John Street, Liverpool, with a basket of flowers, purse, and testimonial, in recognition of her gift, and heroic conduct during and after the disaster. I may add I knew Mr. Harrison as a most careful investigator and a man of scientific tastes and ability.

I select the following case of a mesmeric sensitive

* "Spirits Before Our Eyes," page 215. By W. H. Harrison, 1879.

controlled by a disembodied spirit, from the writings
of Mr. Epes Sargent, author of *"Planchette on the
Despair of Science,"* etc. As appropriately illustrative
of this form of *Clairvoyance:*—

"One of the daughters of my valued correspondent,
the late William Howett, was a mesmeric sensitive.
Howett told Professor W. D. Gunning, whose words
(slightly abridged) I use here, that, on one occasion
his daughter, being entranced, wrote a communication
signed with the name of her brother, supposed to be
in Australia. The import was, that he had been
drowned a few days before in a lake. Dates and details were given. The parents could only wait, as
there was no trans-oceanic telegraph. Months passed,
and at last a letter came from a nephew in Melbourne,
bearing the tidings that their son had been drowned
on such a day, in such a lake, under such and such
circumstances. Date, place, and all the essential details were the same as those given months before
through the daughter. *Mr. Howett believed that the
freed spirit of his son influenced the sister to write;
and I know of no explanation more rational than this."*

Clairvoyance Due To Spiritual Control.

Such cases as the above are the most difficult of all
to prove. What I contend for is, if it is demonstrated
we can control a fellow-being, throw him or her into
a trance state—in which the phenomena of the psychic
state are evolved—and seeing such state is induced
largely by the control of spirit over spirit in the body,
why may not a disembodied spirit control, direct, or
influence a suitable sensitive or medium in the body?
If not, why not? *There is abundant evidence of such
controls.*

Seeing objects concealed in boxes and letters, or
reading books and mottoes, etc., appears to some *Clair-*

voyants to be more difficult than diagnosing disease, or seeing objects at a distance. The why and wherefore seems at first difficult to explain.

The deliberate concealment of objects for the purpose of testing *Clairvoyance* is often the result of a spirit of virulent suspicion, disbelief, and, what is worse, *an earnest desire for failure,* so that the parties may rejoice on the discomfiture of the *Clairvoyants.* With such people failure is a source of pleasure. Nevertheless, seeming impossibilities have been triumphed over. *Long lost wills have been found, and places of the accidental or intentional hiding discovered. In more than one case deliberate fraud has been exposed, and the guilty parties brought to acknowledge the truth of the sensitive's revelations.*

The Fugitive Nature Of Clairvoyance.

"The chief feature," said ˉAlexis Didier, "of the somnambulistic lucidity is it variability. While the conjurer or juggler, at all moments in the day and before all spectators, will invariably succeed, the somnambulist, endowed with the marvellous power of clairvoyance, will not be lucid with all interviewers and at all moments of the day; for the faculty of lucidity being a crisis painful and abnormal, there may be atmospheric influences or invincible antipathies at work opposing its production, and which seem to paralyse all supersensual manifestation. Intuition, clairvoyance, lucidity, are faculties which the somnambulist gets from the nature of his temperament, and which are rarely developed in force." Further, he adds, "the somnambultisic lucidity varies in a way to make one despair; success is continually followed by failure; in a word, error succeeds a truth; but when one analyses the causes of this no right-minded person will bring up the charge of Charlatanism, since the faculty is subject to influences independent of the will and the consciousness of the clairvoyant."

Alexis Didier, like his brother *Adolphe,* was a natural *Clairvoyant,* and excelled in direct and objective clairvoyance, phases of the most striking and convincing character.

Clairvoyance can be cultivated by the aid of *Hyppotnism* and by the introspection process. By the first, the sensitive can be materially assisted by the experience and help of the operator. By the second, natural *Clairvoyance* can be induced. Either processes are more or less suitable to subdue the activity of the senses, and give greater range to the psychic powers. General instructions for using the *"Magic Mirror"* are given in *"A Message For All Mystics,"* which can be obtained free from Messrs. de Laurence, Scott & Co. The operator then knows with whom he has to do, their special temperament and character, what are the best processes to adopt to cultivate their gift, and how far such sensitive students are themselves likely to be suitable for *Clairvoyant* experiments. Many have found the *"Magic Mirror"* or *"The Crystal Gazing"* useful in inducing favorable conditions for the development of *Clairvoyance,* and recommend its use.

CHAPTER IV.

PSYCHOMETRY.

What is psychometry? *Psychometry* is a phase of *Clairvoyance*—the knowledge the psychic obtains by a *clue*, such as a lock of the hair of some absent person, or some portion of a distant object. Mr. Stead calls it (*Review of Reviews,* p. 221, September, 1892) "the strange new science of *Psychometry.*" In this he pardonably errs. *Psychometry* may be strange, but *it* is *not* new. We may not recognise the name as old, but the class of phenomena it specialises is as old as *Clairvoyance* and *Mind-Reading*.

The word *Psychometry* was coined in 1842, to express the character of a new science and art, and is the most pregnant and important word that has been added to the English language. Coined from the Greek (*psyche,* soul; and *metron,* measure), it literally signifies *soul-measuring.*" . . . The *Psychometer* measures the soul.

In the case of *Psychometry,* the measuring assumes a new character, as the object measured and the measuring instrument are the same psychic elements, as measuring power is not limited to the psychic, as it was developed in the first experiments, but has appeared by successive investigations to manifest a wider and wider area of power, until it became apparent that this psychic capacity was really the measure of all things in the universe. Hence, psychometry signifies not merely the measuring of souls and soul capacities, or qualities by our own psychic capacities, but the measurement and judgment of all things conceivable by the human mind; and psychometry means practically *measuring by the soul,* or grasping and estimating all things which are within the range of human intelligence. Psychometry, therefore, is not merely an instrumentality for measuring soul powers, but•a comprehensive agency like mathematics for the solution of many departments of science.

Prophecy is the noblest aspect of *Psychometry,* and there is no reason why it should not become the guiding power to each individual life, and the guiding power of the destiny of nations.

In physiology, pathology, and hygiene, *Psychometry* is as wise and parental as in matters of character and ethics. A competent *Psychometer* appreciates the vital forces, the temperament, the peculiarities, and every departure from the normal state, realising the diseased condition with an accuracy in which external diagnosis often fails. In fact, the natural *Psychometer* is born with a genius for the healing art, and if the practice of medicine were limited to those who possess this power in an eminent degree, its progress would be rapid, and its disgraceful failures in diagnosis and blunders in treatment and prognosis would be less frequently heard of. Many happy tests in diagnosis and in the successful treatment of disease—out of the ordinary routine—are due, in my opinion, not so much to elaborate medical training as to the fact of the practitioner—perhaps unconscious to himself—being possessed of more or less of the psychometric faculty.

Dr. Buchanan,* in his *"Original Sketches,"* gives us

---

* Dr. Joseph Rhodes Buchanan has been Dean and Professor in several American universities. As far back as 1830 he was Professor of Medicine in *Transylvania University.* In the year 1841 he made several important discoveries in cerebral psychology, which he communicated to the American and to the Edinburgh Phrenological Journals. These discoveries are elaborated in his unique system of Anthropology, and are published in his works—*"Therapeutic Sarcognomy," "Psychometry," "The Dawn of a New Civilisation," "System of Anthropology,"* and *"The New Education."*

the history and some details of his discovery, based upon certain investigations of the nervous system. Already he was well versed in the phenomena of hypnotism, which is at this late day becoming a fashionable study and recreation of medical men. He had demonstrated the responsive action of cerebral organs to mesmeric touch and influence, and he was already acquainted with the curious psychological phenomena of sense and thought transference, of double consciousness, and all the nervous and pathological phases peculiar to natural and artificial somnambulism. His investigation for years of the nervous system had clearly shown him that its capacities were far more extensive, varied, and interesting than physiologists and philosophers either knew or were prepared to admit. He found in the nervous system a vast aggregate of powers which constitute the vitality of man, existing in intimate connection with the vast and wonderful powers of his mind. Was it possible or rational to suppose that this nerve-matter, so intimately co-related with mind, and upon which the mind depends for the manifestation of its powers, could be entirely limited to the narrow materialistic sphere assigned by physiologists? He thought not.

In a conversation with Bishop Polk (who afterwards became the celebrated General Polk of Confederate fame), Dr. Buchanan ascertained that Bishop Polk's nervous sensibility was so acute that, if by accident he touched a piece of brass in the night, when he could not see what he had touched, he immediately felt the influence through his system, and recognised an offensive metallic taste.

The discovery of such sensitiveness in one of the most vigorous men, in mind and body, of his day, led Dr. Buchanan to believe that it might be found in many others. It is needless to say his conjecture was correct. Accordingly, in the numerous neurological experiments which he afterwards commenced, he was accustomed to place metals of different kinds in the hands of persons of acute sensibility, for the purpose of ascertaining whether they could feel any peculiar influence, recognise any peculiar taste, or appreciate the difference of metals, by any impression upon their own sensitive nerves. It soon appeared that the power was quite common, and there were a large number of persons who could determine by touching a piece of metal, or by holding it in their hands, what the metal was, as they recognised a peculiar influence proceeding from it, which in a few moments gave them a distinct taste in the mouth. But this sensitiveness was not confined to metallic substances. Every substance possessing a decided taste—sugar, salt, nutmeg, pepper, acid, etc.—appeared to be capable of transferring its influence. The influence appeared to affect the hand, and then travel upwards. He afterwards demonstrated when a galvanic or electric current passed through a medicinal substance, the influence of the substance was transmitted with the current, detected and described by the person operated upon. Medicinal substances, enclosed in paper, were readily recognised and described by their effects. In due time, stranger still, a geological specimen, an article worn, a letter written upon, a photograph which had been handled, a coin, etc., transmitted their influence, and the psychometrist was enabled to read off the history concerning the particular object.

Nearly fifty years have elapsed since the discovery of this "strange new science" and art. "To-day it is widely known, has its respected and competent practitioners, who are able to describe the mental and vital peculiarities of those who visit or write them, and who create astonishment and delight by the fidelity and fulness of the descriptions which they send to persons unknown, and at vast distances. They give minute analysis of character and revelations of particulars *known only to the one described,* pointing out with parental delicacy and tenderness the defects which need correction, or in the perverse and depraved they explain what egotism would deny, but what society, family, and friends recognise to be too true."

PSYCHOMETRIC REFLECTIONS.

A shadow never falls upon a wall without leaving thereupon a permanent trace—a trace made visible by resorting to proper processes. Upon the walls of private apartments, where we think the eye of intrusion is altogether shut out, and our retirement can never be profaned, there exists the vestiges of our acts, *silhouettes of whatever we have done.* It is a crushing thought to whoever has committed secret crime, that the picture of his deed, and the very echo of his words, may be seen and heard countless years after he has gone the way of all flesh, and left a reputation for "respectability" to his children.

Detectives have received impressions from a scene of crime, a clue to the unravelment of the mystery and the detection of the criminal. Yet they could not trace the impressions to anything they saw or heard during their preliminary investigations. No good detective will throw aside such impressions. Indeed, those most successful are those who, while paying attention to all outward and so-called tangible clues, *do not neglect for one moment* the impressions received, and the thoughts *felt,* when gathering information likely to lead to the detection of the lawbreakers. *There are provinces in the mind that physicians have not entered into.*

Thoughts are things—living, real and tangible, images, visions, deep and pungent sensations—which exist in the *Astral Light* after their creation distinct and apart from ourselves—*"Footprints on the sands of time,"* in more senses than one. We all leave our mark in a thousand subtle ways. No material microscope or telescope can detect, nevertheless our mark can be discovered by the powers of the human soul. *From our cradle to the grave*—does it stop there?—every thought, emotion, movement, and action have left their subtle traces, so that our whole life can be traced out by the psychometric expert. We verily give hostages to fortune all through life.

PSYCHOMETRIC SENSITIVES.

Professor Denton was very fortunate in having in his wife, children, and in his sister, Mrs. Cridge, gifted *Psychometers.* His sister possessed this psychic, intuitive faculty in a high degree. Dr. Buchanan was equally fortunate; not only was his wife a first-class sensitive, but he discovered the faculty in several university professors, and in students innumerable. Denton in his travels over America, Europe, and Australia found several hundred good sensitives, some of whom have since made a reputation both in Europe and America for their powers.

One important fact we learn from these pioneers in *Psychometric* research is "that not one of these persons knew they were endowed with the psychometric gift prior to taking part in classes or experiments."

The possession of the faculty is not confined to any age, or to the gentle sex; and, on an average, one female in four and one man in ten are *Psychometric Sensitives.* The possibility is all healthy, sensitive, refined, intuitive, and impressionable persons possess the soul-measuring faculty, and this faculty, like all other innate human powers, can be cultivated and brought to a high stage of perfection.

The *Psychometer*, unlike the induced *Clairvoyant* or *Entranced Medium*, is in general, or outwardly at least, a mere spectator, as one who beholds a drama or witnesses a panorama, and tells in his own way to someone else what he sees and what he thinks about it. The sensitive can dwell on what is seen, examine it closely, and record individual opinions of the impressions of the persons, incidents, and scenes of the long hidden thus brought to light. The sensitive has merely to hold the object in hand or hold it to the forehead (temple), when he or she is enabled to come in contact with the soul of the person or thing with which the object has been in relation. There is no loss of external consciousness, no *"up rush"* of the subliminal, obliterating and overlapping that of common life. The sensitive appears to be in a perfectly normal condition during the whole time of examination, can lay the article down, noticing what takes place, and entering into conversation with those in the room, or drawing subjects, seen or not, as they think best.

WHAT PSYCHOMETRY CAN DO.

I once gave a *Psychometer* a specimen from the carboniferous formation; closing her eyes, she described those swamps and trees, with their tufted heads and scaly trunks, with the great frog-like animals that existed in that age. To my inexpressible delight the key to the ages was in my hands. I concluded that nature had been photographing from the very first. The black islands that floated upon the fiery sea, the gelatinous dots, the first life on our planet, up through everything that flew or swam, had been photographed by Nature, and ten thousand experiments had confirmed the theory. I got a specimen of the lava that flowed from *Kilava,* in *Hawaii,* in 1848. The *Psy-*

chometer by its means described the boiling ocean, the cataract of molten lava that almost equalled Niagara in size. A small fragment of meteorite that fell in Painesville, O., was given to a sensitive who did not then believe in psychometry. This is what she said: "I seem to be travelling away, away, through nothing, right forward. I see what look like stars and mist. I seem to be taken right up; the other specimens took me down." Another sensitive, independently, gave a similar description, but saw it revolving, and its tail of sparks. I took steps to prove that this was not mind reading by wrapping the specimens in paper, shaking them up in a hat, and allowing the sensitive to pick out one and describe it, without anyone knowing which it was. Among them were a fragment of brick from ancient *Rome,* antimony from *Borneo,* silver from *Mexico,* basalt from *Fingal's Cave.* Each place was described correctly by the sensitive in the most minute detail. A fragment from the *Mount of Olives* brought a description of *Jerusalem;* and one from the *Great Pyramid* enabled a young man of Melbourne to name and describe it. A number of experiments from a fragment of *Kent's Cave,* fragments from *Pompeii* and other places brought minute descriptions from the sensitive.

Mr. Stead bears his testimony to *Psychometry.* He gave a shilling to two ladies, at different periods, and unknown to each other. In fact, they were perfect strangers. This shilling, in my mind, had a special story connected with it. The first lady had lived in Wimbledon, and had the profession of being a *Clairvoyante.* To use Mr. Stead's own words, he stated:—
"I took from my purse a shilling which I most prized of all the pieces of money in my possession. I said nothing to her beyond that I had carried it in my pocket for several years. She held the shilling in her hand for some time, and said:—'This carries me back

to a time of confusion and much anxiety, with a feeling that everything depended upon a successful result. This shilling brings me a vision of a very low woman, ignorant and drunken, with whom you had much better have nothing to do. There is a great deal of fever about. I feel great pains, as if I had rheumatic fever in my ankles and joints, but especially in my ankles and my throat. I suffer horribly in my throat; it is an awful pain. And now I feel a coarse, bare hand pass over my brow as distinctly as if you had laid your hand there. It must be her hand. I feel the loss of a child. This woman is brought to me by another. She is about thirty-two years; about five feet high, with dark brown hair, grey eyes, small, nicely-formed nose, large mouth.'" "Can you tell me her name?" asked Mr. Stead. "Not certain, but I think it seems like Annie." "That is all right," said Mr. Stead, and he told her the story of that shilling. About a month afterwards, Mr. Stead tried a Swedish opera singer, who had clairvoyant powers, with the shilling. She pressed it to her brow, and then she told Mr. Stead "she saw a poor woman give him, from her pocket-money, the last shilling she possessed. She has a great admiration for you, she said. She seems to think you have saved her, but she is not *une grande dame*. Indeed, she seems to be a girl of the town." Mr. Stead said:—"I had not spoken a word, or given her the least hint of the story of the shilling." Now, what are the facts? Mr. Stead says that he "was standing his trial at the Old Bailey, a poor outcast girl of the streets, who was dying of a loathsome disease in the hospital, asked that the only shilling that she possessed in the world, might be given to the fund which was being raised in his defence. It was handed to him when he came out of jail, with, 'From a dying girl in hospital, who gives her last shilling,' written on the paper." He (Mr. Stead) has carried it about him ever since, never allowing it to be out of his possession for a single day.

The symptoms which the first *Clairvoyante,* or *Psychometrix,* described were very like those which this poor creature was suffering from in her dying hours. It is too probable that the donor was a low, drunken woman.

These two readings are actually more psychometric than clairvoyant, because, from the clue furnished, they went back and described the conditions and surroundings of the woman who parted with this shilling. They were not thought-readers, because they did not describe what was passing in Mr. Stead's mind. Mr. Stead's experiences fairly illustrate the exercise, in the earlier stages of employment, of the psychometric faculty.

While engaged writing the *"Real Ghost Stories,"* Mr. Stead says:—"My attention was called to a young lady, Miss Catherine Ross, of 41 High Street, Smethwick, Birmingham, who, being left with an invalid sister to provide for, and without other available profession or industry, bethought herself of a curious gift of reading character, with which she seems to have been born, and had subsequently succeeded in earning a more or less precarious income by writing out characters at the modest fee of 5s. You sent her any article you pleased that had been in contact with the object, and she sent you by return a written analysis of the subject's character. I sent her various articles from one person at different times, not telling her they were from the same person. At one time a tuft of hair from his beard, at another a fragment of a nail, and a third time a scrap of handwriting. Each delineation of character differed in some points from the other two, but all agreed, and they were all remarkably correct. When she sent the last she added, 'I don't know how it is, but I feel I have described this person before.' I have tried her since then with locks of hair from persons of the most varied disposition, and have found her wonderfully correct."

"All these things are very wonderful, but the cumulative value of the evidence is too great for any one to pooh-pooh it as antecedently impossible. The chances against it being a mere coincidence are many millions to one."

I believe had this young lady, or others thus endowed, had the training, such as Buchanan, Denton, or other experienced teachers give their pupils, she would make a high class psychometer.

Rev. Minot J. Savage had a paper in a recent number of *The Arena,* on *Psychical Research,* etc., in which he said—"On a certain morning I visited a psychometrist. Several experiments were made. I will relate only one, as a good specimen of what has occurred in my presence more than once. The lady was not entranced or, so far as I could see, in any other than her normal condition. I handed her a letter which I had recently received. She took it, and held it in her right hand, pressing it close, so as to come into as vital contact with it as possible. I had taken it out of its envelope, so that she might touch it more effectively, but it was not unfolded even so much as to give her an opportunity to see even the name. It was written by a man whom she had never seen, and of whom she had never heard. After holding it a moment she said, 'This man is either a minister or a lawyer; I cannot tell which. He is a man of a good deal more than usual intellectual power. And yet he has never met with any success in life as one would have expected, considering his natural ability. Something has happened to thwart him and interfere with his success. At the present time he is suffering with severe illness and mental depression. He has pain here' (putting her hand to the back of her head, at the base of the brain).

"She said much more, describing the man as well as I could have done it myself. But I will quote no more, for I wish to let a few salient points stand in clear outline. These points I will number, for the sake of clearness :—

1. "She tells me he is a man, though she has not even glanced at the letter."

2. "She says he is either a minister or a lawyer; she cannot tell which. No wonder, for he was both; that is, he had preached for some years, then he had left the pulpit, studied law, and at this time was not actively engaged in either profession."

3. "She speaks of his great natural ability. This was true in a most marked degree."

4. "But he had not succeeded as one would have expected. This again was strikingly true. Certain things had happened—which I do not feel at liberty to publish—which had broken off his career in the middle and made his short life seem abortive."

About eighteen years ago a lady in Swansea sent me a lock of hair, and asked me to send her my impressions. I did so, which I remember were not pleasant. I informed her, as near as my recollection now serves, that the person to whom the hair belonged was seriously ill. No earthly skill could do anything for him. Diagnosing the character of the insidious disease which was then undermining a once powerful and active organisation, I felt constrained to add he *would live six weeks.* I held the envelope, with its contents, in my left hand, and wrote the impressions as they came with my right. I remember hesitating about sending the letter, but eventually sent it. The accuracy of my diagnosis, description of the patient, and the fulfilment of the prophecy as to his death were substantiated in a Swansea paper, *The Bat.* The patient was no other than Captain Hudson, the British master mariner who sailed the first ship on teetotal principles from a British port, and who subsequently became one of the most powerful of British mesmerists. The lady who sent the lock of hair was his wife, and the lady who contributed the letter to the papers was his widow.

LESSONS IN PSYCHOMETRY.

How To Develop The Psychometric Faculty.

Class Experiments.—The sensitives are not to be magnetised or unduly influenced by positive manner and suggestions, but are to sit in their normal state (and without mental effort or straining to find out what they have in their hands), and simply give expression to their impressions—sensations, tastes, etc., if any, and no matter how strange to them these may be. Let the experimenter or operator place different metallic substances in their hands, taking care that these substances are carefully covered with tissue paper or other light substance, which will help to hide their character, and at the same time not prevent their influence being imparted, or try them with medical substances. In those sufficiently sensitive, an emetic will produce a feeling of nausea. The substance must be put down before it causes vomiting. Geological specimens can be given—a shell, a tooth, or tusk. Let the experimenter record the utterances patiently, and seek confirmation of the description from an examination of the specimen subsequently. He should not know what special specimen it is previous to the psychometer's declared opinion. Good specimens are best. Thus a fragment of pottery, a piece of scori, or a bit of brick from, say, Pompeii would present material from which the psychometrist could glean strong and vivid impressions.

If a medical man is not satisfied as to the correct pathological conditions of his patient, he might ask the psychometer to take some article of the patient in hand, and get, in the sensitive's own—and therefore very likely untechnical—language, what he feels and sees regarding this particular patient's case. Unsuspected abscesses and tumors have been correctly pointed out in this way.

In the same way a correct diagnosis of character can be given in many instances more correctly, more subtle, and penetrating in detail, than estimates built upon mere external and physical signs of temperament and cranial contours.

Lay a coin on a polished surface of steel. Breathe upon it, and all the surface will be affected save the portion on which the coin lay. In a few minutes neither trace of breathing nor of the coin is likely to be seen on the surface of the polished steel. Breathe again, and the hitherto unseen image of the coin is brought to light. In like manner, everything we touch records invisibly to us that action. Hand your sensitive a letter which has been written in love or joy, grief or pungent sorrow, and let them give expression to their sensations. As the breath brought back the image on the steel, so will the nervous and the psychic impressionability of the sensitive bring to light the various emotions which actuated the writers who penned the letters. I have brushed the surface of the polished plate with a camel's-hair brush, yet on breathing upon it the image of the coin previously laid upon it was distinctly visible. The mere casual handling of letters by intermediates will not obliterate the influence of the original writers; they have permeated the paper with their influence, so that, if a score or more of *Psychometrists* held the paper, they would coincide perhaps not in their language, but in their descriptions of the originals and the state of their minds while writing.

The experimenter may help, by asking a few judicious but not leading questions, to direct and guide the attention of the *Psychometrist*. The description will be a capital delineation of the individual who wrote the letter. We have frequently tested the sincerity of correspondents, real and other friends, by this process. If the results have sometimes been unpleasant revelations, we have yet to find in any case that we have been mistaken. How is the sensitive able to glean so much of the real character of the original? one is inclined to ask. While writing, sincerity and earnestness leave a deeper impression than indifference, pretence, or ordinary come-to-tea politeness. Some letters are instinct with the writer's identity, individuality, masculinity, earnestness, and enthusiasm. Others are lacking in these things, because the writers were devoid of these qualities, while others vary at different times. The writer writes as *his soul* moves him, and the writing expresses his aims and hopes as they appear to his external consciousness. While writing, *his soul* draws his image on the paper, and pictures out thereon his real thoughts; and when the sensitive gets hold of the letter, outstands the image of the writer and the imagery of his thoughts. The psychic consciousness of the psychometer grasps the details and describes them.

The strange science of psychometry is of profound interest to all. *Psychometers* are to be found in every household. The whole subject is one about which a good deal more could be easily written, but this must do.

Those who desire to understand *Psychometry* cannot do better than read up fully the literature of the subject, and those who desire to practise *Psychometry* may do much to ascertain whether they possess the faculty in any degree; but all are warned to have nothing to do with cheap so-called Professors who undertake to *develop* their powers, a *self-evident absurdity*.

CHAPTER V.

THOUGHT-TRANSFERENCE AND MENTAL TELEPATHY.

Thought-Transference is a phase of *"psychic perception."* In some respects it bears a greater relation to feeling than sight. It is distinguished from pure *Clairvoyance* by the result of experiment. For instance, suppose I had in the Rothesay case designed M. C., the *Clairvoyante*, should see "a maid in the room, dressed in a black dress, with neat white collar and cuffs, wearing a nicely-trimmed white apron, and a white tulle cap with bows and streamers, or that a black-and-white spotted cat lay comfortably coiled upon the hearth-rug, or some other strongly projected mental image." Now, suppose while M. C. was examining the room, she declared she *saw* the maid, and described her, or the cat, or other objects projected from my mind, and described these, then this would be a case of *Thought-Transference.*

There is a distinction between *Thought-Transference* and *Thought-Reading.* It is no mere fanciful distinction either. *Thought-Transference* occurs when the ideas, thoughts, and emotions of one mind are projected by intense action and received by the sensitive and impressionable mind of another—*awake or asleep is immaterial*—so long as it occurs without pre-arrangement and contact.

Telepathy is a more vivid form of sudden and unexpected thought-transference, in which the intense thoughts and wishes of one person, more or less in sympathy, are suddenly transferred to the consciousness of another. The thoughts transmitted are often so intense as to be accompanied by the vision of the person, and by the sound of their voice.

Telepathy bears about the same relation to *Thought-Transference as "second sight" does to Clairvoyance.* *Thought-Transference* and *Clairvoyance* can be cultivated. Not so *Telepathy and Second Sight.* They are phenomena, which belong to the unexpected, portents of the unusual, or sudden revelations of what is, and what is about to happen. Doubtless, there are conditions more favorable than others for inception of these. One needs to be *"in a quiet spirit"* before *Telepathic* and *Second Sight* messages are secured. Hence it is noticed *Telepathic* revelations mostly come in the quietude of the evening, just before sleep, between sleep and waking, and under similar conditions favourable to passivity and receptivity in the sensitive or percipient.

In *Thought-Reading* both operator and sensitive are aware that something is to be done, and indications, intentional or otherwise, are given to make the thought-reader find out what is required. More or less sensitiveness is required in both phases. In *Telepathy* and *Thought-Transference* the psychic elements are in the ascendency; in *Thought-Reading* they may be more or less present, but intention, sensitiveness, and muscular contact are adequate enough, I think, to account for the phenomena, as witnessed at public entertainments —so far, at least, as these entertainments are genuine.

How do we think? what are thoughts? and how are thoughts transferred? are reasonable questions, and merit more elaborate solution than is possible in an elementary work like this.

We think in pictures; words are but vehicles of thought. In *Thought-Transference* we can successfully project actions, or a series of actions, by forming in our minds a scene or picture of what is done and what is to be reproduced. When, however, we think of a sentence consisting of few or many words, there is nothing more difficult to convey. Words belong to our external life here, and are but arbitrary expressions and signs for what in the internal or soul-life is flashed telepathically from mind to mind.

Thoughts are things for good or ill, veritable and living realities, apart from our exterior selves, independent of words. The more words, often the less thought. Try to teach a child by the slow, dry-as-dust method of words, and the road to knowledge is hard and wearisome. Convey the same thoughts by illustrations and experiments, and the child's mind at once grasps the ideas we desire to convey.

Thoughts are living entities (how poor are words!) which our own souls have given birth to, or created in the intensity of our love, wisdom, or passion. The Eastern *Adepts* teach, "A good thought is perpetuated as an active, beneficent power, an evil one as a malignant demon. The *Hindoo* calls this *Karma*. The *Adept* evolves these shapes consciously; other men throw them off unconsciously." How true in our experience! *The thoughts of some men blast, while those of others bless. There is wisdom in thinking deliberately, intelligently, and therefore conscientiously, not passionately, impulsively, or carelessly.*

In *Thought-Transference* the reproduction of exact words and dates seems to be most difficult. Indeed, the transmission of arbitrary words and signs is apparently the most difficult. The reason, I conclude, is, ideas belong to our inner, real, and spiritual life, and names, words, and dates to our exterior existence. The ideas can be expressed in the language of the sensitive, according to culture or the want of it. If the true lineaments of the picture are given, need we be too exacting as to the special frame surrounding the picture?

Notwithstanding the difficulty in transference and the reading of the exact words, this has also been frequently done. A very high state of receptivity and sensitiveness, however, is necessary in the percipient. An incident of exact word-reading is related by Gerald Massey, the distinguished philosopher and poet. Mr. Massey met Mr. Home at the London terminus just on his (Mr. Massey's) arrival from Hertfordshire. Home and he entered into conversation, during which Home suddenly said "he hoped Mr. Massey would go on with his poem."

"What did he mean?" asked Mr. Massey.

"The poem," replied Home, "you composed four lines of just now in the train."

This was surprising to Mr. Massey, who had actually composed, but had not written, the four lines of a new poem on the journey. Mr. Massey challenged Mr. Home to repeat the lines, which Home did word for word.

How are thoughts transferred? No one can positively say. There are theories enough—the *theory of brain-waves* and of *a universal impalpable elastic ether*, of *undulating* motions, or other more or less materialistic hypothesis.*

---

* Thought is accompanied by molecular vibrations in the grey matter of the brain, and these brain molecules, like everything else, are immersed in and interpenetrated by ether; this being so, their vibrations must set up wave-motions in the ether, and they must spread out from the brain in all directions. Further, these brain-waves, or thought waves, being thus sent out into space, will produce some phenomena, and, reasoning by analogy, we may expect that—as in the case of sound-waves—sympathetic vibrations will be set up in bodies similar to that which generates the waves, if those bodies are attuned to respond. Again, reasoning by analogy, we may expect—as in electric resonance—that such oscillations would be set up as are found when electric waves are sent out and, meeting a circuit in consonance with them, set up in that circuit oscillations like their own.

In view of these facts, which are well ascertained, it does not seem improbable that a brain engaged in intense thought should act as a centre for thought-radiation, nor that these radiations,

We know there are no psychic phenomena without their corresponding physical correlatives, and, in this life at least, these are in thoughts evolved without producing corresponding molecular changes in the brain. We notice the human brain is capable of being, and is, acted upon daily by much less subtle influences than mental impressions. . We can appreciate light impinged upon our cerebral centres at the rate of millions of undulations, and sound as the result of 20,000 to 30,-000 vibrations per second. So, sensitives, when in the mesmeric or psychic states, are readily acted upon, and respond as in thought-transference to our thoughts and sensations, and veritably read our minds, because of the *rapport* or sympathy thus established. Whether they become percipients of the nervous-vibrations which escape from our own sensorums or not, what does it matter *if they can, as they frequently do,* read our minds?

A means of illustrating sympathy: If a sounding board is placed so as to resound to all instruments of an orchestra, and connected by a metallic rod of considerable length with the sounding-board of a harp or piano, the instrument will accurately repeat the notes transmitted.

The nervous system, in its two-fold relation to the physical and spiritual being, is inconceivably more finely organised than the most perfect instrument, and is possessed of finer sensitiveness.

---

proceeding outwards in all directions, should affect other brains on which they fall, provided that these other brains are tuned to vibrate in unison with them.

Light waves are etheric vibrations, and it would seem that these brain-waves should *"partake of the nature of light."* If so, why should it not be possible to obtain, say, by means of a lens, a photographic impression of them?

Such a thought-record suitably employed might be able to awaken at any subsequent time in the brain of a person submitting himself to its influence thoughts identical to those recorded.

It must not be inferred that all minds are equally receptive. The Hindoo Masters teach that: Light falls on all substances alike, but is very differently affected by each substance. *One class of bodies absorb all but the yellow rays, another all but the blue, another all but the red, because these substances are so organised that they respond only to the waves of the colors reflected.*

All persons do not hear alike. They receive certain sounds and are deaf to all others, although the sound-waves strike all tympanums alike. *All persons do not see alike.* Some perceive colors, others cannot distinguish between one color and another, or can only see the more striking colors—fineness of shade they do not perceive. So there are individuals who cannot receive mental impressions, unless, indeed, they are conveyed in the baldest and most esoteric manner. In a word to convey and receive impressions they must be sent along the line of the least resistance, that of *true sympathy.* These must be one mind adequate to the projection, and another mind sufficiently sensitive to receive and record the thoughts projected.

TRANSFERENCE OF TASTE IN THE MESMERIC STATE.

The operator will slowly eat or taste half-a-dozen lozenges or sweets of different flavours, and the subject or sensitive most in sympathy with him will also in imagination eat of and describe the taste of the various sweets. Concerning which he has no other knowledge than the thoughts of eating and tasting, which are transmitted to him from the brain of the operator. The mere eating of the lozenges by the operator, without his being fully aware of the fact, will deepen the impression on the operator's mind, and help to concentrate his energies for the transmission of his ideas or mental suggestions to his subject.

A step or two further and we find with greater sensitiveness the sensitives can read the thoughts of the operator, whether the thoughts were transmitted intentionally or not.

We are compelled to acknowledge that certain emanating undulations from the sensorium can generate different series of thoughts, and that the trembling organisation, or parts of it, can, by flinging or throwing off distinct or particular pulsatory waves, inoculate or produce like vibrations in another person's brain, making up in it identical thoughts, following by like feelings, and often in this way, perhaps, capable of inciting, *through sympathy,* like enactments of deeds and pursuits.

THOUGHT-TRANSFERENCE IN DREAMS.

The following interesting letter appeared in *The Phrenological Magazine* (p. 260, April, 1890), and as I know of the *bona-fides* of the writer, I have much pleasure in reproducing it:

"DEAR SIR: This morning, at a little before four o'clock, I awoke as the outcome of great mental distress and grief through which I had just passed in a dream, my body trembling and in a cold perspiration. I had been walking with my little boy, aged five and a-half years, and some friends. A heavy rain overtaking us, we stood up for shelter; and venturing forth into a maze of streets, I missed my two friends, who, threading among people, had turned into a side street without my noticing. Looking for them, my boy slipped from me, and was lost in the crowd. I became bewildered by the strange labyrinth of streets and turnings, and quickly taking one of them which gave an elevated position, I looked down on the many windings, but could nowhere see my boy. It was to me an unknown locality, and, running down among the people, I was soon sobbing aloud in my distress, and calling out the name of the child, when I awoke. With wakefulness came a sense of relief and thankfulness. Gladly realising that the whole was only a dream, and still scarcely awake, I was startled by a cry of terror and pain from an adjoining bedroom—such a cry as could not be left unheeded. It came from the same child, and pierced me with a distinct sense of pain. I was immediately by his side. My voice calmed him. 'I thought I was lost' was all he could say, and doubtless he was soon composed and asleep again. To me the coincidence was too remarkable and without parallel in my own experience. Later on, at breakfast, the child gave further his dream that he *had been out with me and was lost.* I am only familiar with such things in my reading. Dr. DE LAWRENCE'S article in last month's *Phrenological Magazine* (page 143) mentions that, 'when the *Prince Imperial* died from assegai thrusts in Zululand, his mother in England felt the intensity of his thoughts at the time, felt the savage lance pierce her own side, and knew or felt at the time that she was childless.' But I am not of the *spirituelle* type, with only a thin parchment separation between this life of realities and the great beyond, of those who, privileged to live in close touch with the future, are the subjects of premonitions and warnings. My spirituality 4 to 5 and reflectives 6 point rather the other way, but I shall, nevertheless, hold tight to the lad. What is the underlying cause of the coincidence? Which of the two minds influenced the other, if either?"—Yours Truly,

G. COX.

In this case of *Thought-Transference,* I am inclined to the opinion that the father's mind influenced that of the boy, the son being the more sensitive of the two. Mr. Cox dreamt an ordinary but pretty vivid dream, which aroused from its nature vivid and intense anxiety on his part. A similar train of thought was awakened in the child. If thought-transference occurs in waking life, why not in sleep, when, as abundant telepathic instances testify, the phenomenon is of most frequent occurrence.

THOUGHT-TRANSFERENCE AT SEA.

The percipient was Captain G. A. Johnson, of the schooner "August H. Johnson." He had sailed from Quero for home. On the voyage he encountered a terrible hurricane. On the second day he saw a disabled brig, and near by a *barque*. He was anxious to reach home, and, thinking the barque would assist the brig, continued on.

But the impression came that he must turn back and board the brig. He could not shake it off, and at last he, with four men, boarded the brig in a dory. He found her deserted, and made sail in her. After a time they saw an object ahead, appearing like a man on a cake of ice. The dory was again manned, and set to the rescue. It proved to be the mate of the barque *"Leawood"* clinging to the bottom of an overturned boat, which, being white, appeared in the distance as ice.

The Captain's sensitiveness may have been aroused by the exhaustion of so much wakefulness and care during the length of the storm, the sight of the derelict and deserted brig; at the same time the premonitions were opposed to his own desire and anxiety to get home.

THOUGHT-TRANSFERENCE FROM THE DYING TO THE
LIVING IN A DREAM.

*The following by E. Ede, M. D., of Guilford (J. S.
P. R., July, 1882):*

"Lady G. and her sister had been spending the
evening with their mother, who was in her usual health
and spirits when they left her. In the middle of the
night the sister awoke in a fright, and said to her husband, 'I must go to my mother at once; do order the
carriage. I am sure she is ill.' The husband, after
trying in vain to convince his wife that it was only a
fancy, ordered the carriage. As she was approaching
the house, where two roads met, she saw lady G.'s
carriage. When they met, each asked the other why
she was there. The same reply was made by both—'I
could not sleep, feeling sure my mother was ill, and so
I came to see.' As they came in sight, they saw their
mother's confidential maid at the door, who told them
when they arrived that their mother had taken suddenly ill, and was dying, and had expressed an earnest
wish to see her daughters."

The percipients having been so lately in company
and sympathy with their mother possibly rendered
them more susceptible to her influence.

THOUGHT-TRANSFERENCE FROM THE DEAD TO THE
LIVING IN A DREAM.

*Related by Mr. Myers, page 208, Proceedings
S. P. R., July 1892:*

"About March, 1857, Mrs. Mennier, in England,
dreamt that she saw her brother, whose whereabouts
she did not know, standing headless at the foot of the
bed with his head lying in a coffin by his side. The

dream was at once mentioned. It afterwards appeared that at about the time the head of the brother seen, Mr. Wellington, was actually cut off by the Chinese at Sarawak." On this case, Mr. Gurney remarks— "This dream, if it is to be telepathically explained, must apparently have been due to the last flash of thought in the brother's consciousness. It may seem strange that a definite picture of his mode of death should present itself to a man in the instant of receiving an unexpected and fatal blow; but, as Hobbes said, 'Thought is quick.' The coffin, at any rate, may be taken as an item of death-imagery supplied by the dreamer's mind."

"We have now, however," says Mr. Myers, "seen a letter from Sir James Brookes (*Rajah of Sarawak*), and an extract from the *Straits Times* of March 21st, 1857, in the (London) *Times* for April 29th, 1857, which makes it, I think, quite conceivable that the dream was a reflection of knowledge acquired after death, and the head on the coffin had a distinct meaning." Sir James Brookes says: "Poor Wellington's remains were consumed [by the Chinese]; his head, borne off in triumph, alone attesting his previous murder." The *Straits Times* says: "The head was given up on the following day. The head, therefore, and the head alone, must have been buried by Mr. Wellington's friends; and its appearance in the dream *on the coffin*, with a headless body standing beside it, is a coincidence even more significant than the facts which Mr. Gurney had before him when he wrote."

The transmission of thought from a spirit discarnate to one incarnate, whose body was asleep, should not be esteemed impossible. Abundant instances, equally well substantiated, might be recorded did space permit.

Thought Transference In Prayer.

This may be a common experience, but only once in my life have I had conscious knowledge of anything so remarkable. For some years before devoting my attention to these subjects, I resided in Liverpool, and had been a member of the Zion Methodist Church, or Chapel, in Everton, and in time was duly placed on the local preachers' plan. In this capacity I became acquainted with a worthy old man—a chapel-keeper, who looked after the meeting house situated in —— street. He had been an old soldier, and possessed something of the faith of the Roman centurion. Poor in the things of this world, he was rich in the sublimity of his love to God and the nobility and purity of his life. I never think of "*Old Daddy Walker*" but his character and this incident comes to my mind, viz.: One morning I was hurrying down West Derby Road to business, and, indeed had got halfway down Brunswick Road, when I commenced to think about old Walker (I had not seen or thought of him for some months). I attempted to throw aside my impressions, as passing thoughts. No use. I became worried about him, and was asking myself questions. "Was he ill?" "Maybe, he is in want?" "I think I will hurry back and see?" I had not much time to spare. It would consume fully twenty minutes to walk back. After hesitating, I went up Brunswick Road and up West Derby Road, and to —— Street, and tapped at the door of his house. There was no response. The street door was slightly ajar. I went in, and found the old pair on their knees in the kitchen. He was engaged in earnest prayer. After kindly salutations, I apologised for intruding, and told him, as I went to business, "I had been bothered about him in my mind, and did not feel satisfied until I had seen him, and knew the truth." He told me, as near as I can recollect, "He was at his last extremity. There was no food or fuel in the house, he had no money. and he had been putting the whole case before the Lord." I had half a sovereign about me, which I had taken out of the house for an entirely different purpose. This I gave to him. The old man, rubbing a tear from his eye, looking at his wife, said: "Mary, don't thee doubt the Lord anymore. I said He would help, and He has given me what I asked for." Old Walker went on to explain, not only his bad fix, but that he had no money to buy firewood with. He meant that he bought up old wood and tar-barrels, which he cut up into lengths and made into bundles, and sold for firewood; and that he had asked the Lord for ten shillings, as he wanted that sum to buy a certain lot which could be obtained for that amount. The old man obtained what he asked for. He believed the Lord had answered his prayer.

Thought Transmission In Prayer.

Since writing the above, the following came under my notice. *In the J. S. P. R., May, 1885, Dr. Joseph Smith, Warrington, England, says:*

"I was sitting one evening reading, when a voice came to me, saying: 'Send a loaf to James Grady's.' I continued reading, and the voice continued with greater emphasis, and this time it was accompanied with an irresistible impulse to get up. I obeyed, and went into the village and brought a loaf of bread, and, seeing a lad at the shop door, I asked him if he knew James Grady. He said he did, so I bade him carry it and say a gentleman sent it. Mrs. Grady was a member of my class, and I went next morning to see what came of it, when she told me a strange thing happened her last night. She said she wished to put the children to bed, they began to cry for want of food, and she had nothing to give them. She then went to prayer, to ask God to give them something. Soon after which the lad came to the door with the loaf. I calculated, on inquiry, that the prayer and the voice I heard exactly coincided in point of time."

> "More things are wrought by prayer
> Than this world dreams of."

Those who know anything of Methodism, will know this. The Methodists have a profound faith in prayer, and also there is a very close relationship between a class-leader and his members. Dr. Smith was, therefore, all the more likely to be the percipient of the woman's earnest and intense prayer to God to feed her hungry children. The Infinite must have an infinite variety of ways of fulfilling His own purposes. Is it unreasonable to suppose that prayer to Him may not be answered indirectly "through means?" and that thought-transference, as in this instance, may be one of the means? If not, why not?

Charitable institutions are maintained; orphans saved, reared, and educated; missions of mercy organised, and the necessary means found by the agency of prayer. Beside "the angels," in That sphere just beyond the ken of the physical, may not our waves of thought, projected by prayer, be impinged upon, and directly affect susceptible minds in this world, by directing their attention to those works of faith and goodness? Prayer is the language of love, and the outcome of true helplessness and need. *A praying man is an earnest man. In prayer thoughts are things—bread upon the waters.*

THOUGHT TRANSFERENCE IN DISTRESS.

I withhold the names for family reasons. Mr.——
had been in business in Glasgow for nearly thirty years,

and, from comparatively small beginnings, had been very successful. Latterly, he and his family resided in ———, a suburb of Glasgow. Both in the city and in this district Mr. ——— was very much respected, being a church member and holding office in ——— Free Church. For some time Mr. ——— had been ailing, and his medical attendent advised him to take a sea voyage —a thorough change, etc. In compliance with this advice, he took a trip up the Mediterranean. Miss ———, a distant relative of his, had been visiting Glasgow, and, being on terms of intimacy with the family, knew of his departure from Glasgow. About two weeks after he left, she also left Glasgow for Edinburgh. While in the train for Edinburgh, she was overcome with great anxiety for Mrs. ———, his wife. Unable to shake the feeling off, instead of going to Edinburgh, she actually got out of the train halfway, at Falkirk, and took the next train back to Glasgow, and went to her friend's house, whom she found in great distress. Mrs. ——— had, about the time Miss ——— became distressed in the train, received word that her husband was found dead (having committed suicide) in his berth on the steamer at *Constantinople*. The state of mind of the newly-made widow re-acted on that of Miss ———. As Miss ——— was not only a dear friend, but was noted for her earnest piety, the widow at once earnestly desired to see her. When last these two friends saw each other, everything seemed to contribute to happiness and comfort. Mrs. ——— was looking forward hopefully for the return of her husband, restored in health, to herself and children.

Thought Transference In Ordinary Experience.

Whether *Thought-Transference* is a "relic of a decaying faculty," or the "germ of a new and fruitful sense," daily experience in the lives of most furnish abundant evidence of the existence of such a power. My own life, while in *India,* has supplied me with abundant evidence of the fact. It is a common occurrence with us for either my *Disciples* or I to utter or give expression to the thoughts, which, for the time being, occupied the conscious plane in the other. It is possible there may have been, as there has been in some instances, some half phrase uttered or manner shown, which in the one have aroused the thoughts expressed by the other.

Another experience is the anticipation of letters and their contents. This is most frequent in the morning, just before rising. I frequently see the letters and the shape of the envelope and style of address before I actually see the letters on my consulting table.

The most common experience of all is recognised by the adage, *"Think of the Devil, and he will appear."* I have noted this in particular. Sitting at the table, there is "popped" into my mind a thought of someone. I will remark, "I think Mr. or Mrs. —— will be here to-day," and they come. Certainly, all who have come in this way have been students or friends; and although they appear subsequent to the thought of them, the evidence in favor of *Thought-Transference* may not be esteemed conclusive. I say it is a common experience. I don't think we should despise any experience, because it is common. To be common, indicates there is a basis, amounting to a psychic law, to account for its existence.

Another common experience is the crossing of letters. One person suddenly recollects "So-and-so;" and writes them a letter excusing delay in writing, retailing news, and in all probability writing on some subject more particularly than on others. Strange to say, the person you have written to has also been engaged writing to you about the same time and on similar subjects. Both have possibly posted their letters at such a time that the delivery has been crossed. I do not say this proves anything; yet I cannot help thinking the experience is too frequent to be accounted for by the usual explanation of accident or coincidence.

Mark Twain's article on *"Mental Telegraphy"* is fresh in the minds of most magazine readers. Whether that article had a basis in the writer's actual experience or not, it is a pretty common experience with most literary men.

"Distance," says Mr. Tuttle, "has inappreciable influence on the *Transference* of thought. It may take place in the same room, or where the two persons are thousands of miles apart. As a personal experience, I will relate one of many similar incidents which have awakened my attention to this wonderful phenomenon. Sitting by my desk one evening, suddenly as a flash of light, the thought came to write an article for the *Harbinger of Light,* published at *Melbourne, Australia.* I had, by correspondence, become acquainted with the editor, W. H. Terry, but there had been no letters passed for many a year. I had not thought of him, or his journal for I do not know how long a time, and I was amused at first with the idea of writing on the subject suggested. But the impression was so strong that I prepared and forwarded an article. Nearly two months passed before I received a letter from *Mr. Terry,* requesting me to write an article on the subject on which I have written; and, making due allowance for time, the dates of our letters were the same. In our experience, this crossing of letters answering each other has twice occurred—the second by *Mr. Terry* answering a request of mine."

Dr. Charles W. Hidden, of Newburyport, Mass., U. S. A., reports a somewhat similar experience to that of *Mark Twain* and the above, which was reported in a recent number of the *Religio Philosophical Journal:*

A very peculiar plot impressed itself upon his mind,

and he immediately based a story upon the plot. He read the story to his family, and was about to send it to a publication to which his wife had recently become a subscriber. When the next number arrived he opened it to learn how to forward his *manuscript*, and great was his surprise to find on the first page a story bearing the title of his own, and a plot almost identical with that which he had written. Parts of the published article appeared word for word. It is needless to add that *Dr. Hidden* tossed his *manuscript* into his desk, and it is there yet. His explanation is, that he caught the title and the plot from another, just as *Mark Twain* caught the plot of the *"Big Bonanza"* from his friend *Simmons.*

It would be nigh impossible to illustrate the various phases of *Thought-Transference,* ranging, as they do, from the association of ideas which may be aroused by a hint, a half-uttered word, or a gesture, to the unmistakable facts of pure *Mental Transference,* and, higher still, to the region of pure psychism, where spirit influences inspire and direct spirit, and thought-bodies are no longer recognised as mere subjective spirits but living and tangible objective personalities, albeit discarnate.

We can say truly with the *Hindoo Sages,* *"There is a power that acts within us, without consulting us."*

CHAPTER VI.

THOUGHT-READING EXPERIMENTS.

Having given satisfactory evidence of the reality of *Thought-Transference,* I propose in this CHAPTER to show how this can be done, and how to give *Thought-Reading* entertainments.

Experimental *Mind-Reading* may be distinguished, for the sake of study, as the *abnormal,* the *normal,* and the *spurious.*

The *abnormal,* that which takes place in *trance, dream, vision,* or which may be the product of artificial somnambulism or of some super-sensitive condition of the nervous system, through disease. We observe *Thought-Transference* in these conditions, rather than attempt to cultivate it.

The *normal,* where the phenomena takes place in the ordinary waking state, *without muscular contact.*

The *spurious, Mind-Reading* so-called, as the result of musculation or *contact,* but which is, in fact, only muscle-reading.

In both the *abnormal* and *normal,* direct transference of thought from mind to mind can only take place when there is the necessary development of psychic activity in the agent or operator, and the equally necessary sensitiveness in the sensitive or percipient.

Classed under *Muscle-Reading* are those performances and games in which the sensitive reads not the mind, but some special desire (of those with whom he or she may be placed *in contact*), by a "careful study of the indications unconsciously given by the agent or operator to the percipient or reader."

86

In both *abnormal* and *normal Thought-Reading,* then, are presented innumerable instances of the possession of psychic faculties; in the muscle-reading phase there may be, and it is possible all successful *"readers"* have, more or less sensitiveness, to take impressions.

To cultivate *Mind-Reading* in a sensitive, the operator should first cultivate in himself the habit of projecting mental pictures, and think of things as seen by the eye, rather than as described by words. This is best done by calling to mind a landscape or domestic scene, by conceiving and mentally building up the same, and, by degrees, getting each feature or detail well stamped in his mind.

It is well in the beginning of these experiments to make the scene as simple, and yet as natural and as complete in detail, as possible. For instance, let the operator think of such a picture as this: A bright little landscape, having a well-defined cottage on the left, just on the margin of a small lake; boat with two figures in the foreground; rising bank upon the right; and a little higher up a defined windmill, well thrown out by the perspective of blue-ridged and undulating mountains, and sky in the background.

The agent, having satisfied himself of his sensitive's whole or partial powers of psychic perception, might ask: *"Do you see anything now?"* and quickly and deliberately go to work, meanwhile formulating definitely such a picture as the above; even allowing himself to get into ecstacies over the scene—peopling the cottage and the mill, and introducing imaginary conversation between the individual dwellers therein, and so on. The sensitive will describe the whole as the same is *felt* or perceived. This experiment may appear to some to be impossible, but the word impossible belongs to the limitations of sense, and not to the range of the things possible to the human spirit.

Some sensitives and mediums take impressions from their surroundings—their *Clairvoyant* revelations are often nothing more than so much *Mind-Reading*. *Nothing More;* but this nothing more is a great deal. Certainly, it may not prove the existence of spirit, apart from the sensitive's own powers; but it does prove that man has other avenues of knowledge than those which he is usually credited.

The development of *Mind-Reading* in the psychic states may be encouraged by a little judicious assistance or direction. Invite the sensitive to pay attention to So-and-so; to visit places, to examine rooms, or describe people whom the sensitive has never seen. But the places, the rooms, and the persons must be *distinctly in the minds* of those persons, or agents, with whom he or she is placed in *rapport*.

During these experiments the sensitive will say, *"I see this,"* or describe that other, as if he actually saw. Hence the infinitely close relationship of mind-reading to clairvoyance. Thought-*Reading in Spiritualism will be referred to in the next chapter.*

Once possessing a good sensitive, the development of the power, as a matter of fact, lies particularly in the operator's ability to concentrate and focus his thoughts—to think clearly, calmly, vividly, and distinctly himself—*and to deliberately and conscientiously project the same.*

THE NORMAL EXPERIMENTS WITHOUT CONTACT.

An idle hour or so can be profitably filled up on a long winter's evening with experiments in *Mind-Reading,* without resorting to mesmerism. It will be found that there are *Mind-Readers* in every family—some boy, girl, or young woman more sensitive than the rest to impressions.

Sometimes it has been found, when two or more persons think of the same object, as in the *"willing game,"* the impression becomes more vivid, and the sensitive finds, or describes, the article, or thing, more easily. It has been left to the versatility of Professor Lodge, of the *University College, Liverpool,* to project two distinct images at the same time to a sensitive. He requested two friends to look at a paper that he had given to each. On one paper a square was drawn, and on the other an oblique cross. Neither person knew what the other was looking at, and after they had looked intently at these diagrams for a short time, the sensitive, who was in a normal condition, but blindfold, said: "I see two figures—first I see one, and then, below that, another. I do not know which I am to draw. I cannot see either plainly." Having been requested to draw what she saw, she drew a square, with an oblique cross inside of it. On being questioned, she replied that she did not know why she placed the cross in the square. The two images projected by distinct minds, intermingled, and were produced, as narrated by Professor Lodge. We can readily see that confusion will arise where a number of persons are thinking of different subjects, or when some positive minded individual declared mind-reading to be an impossibility.

Something after the above experiments of Professor Lodge are those which were conducted by Mr. Guthrie, a London barrister, and reported by him to the *Society of Psychical Research.*

A number of diagrams, roughly drawn off-hand at the time, were shown to the agent or precipitant, Mr. G., the subject, or percipient, a lady, being blind-fold. During the process of transference, the agent looked steadily and in silence at the drawing, the subject meanwhile sitting opposite to him, and behind the stand on which the drawing lay, so that it was entirely

RESULTS OF EXPERIMENTS IN THOUGHT-TRANSFERENCE.

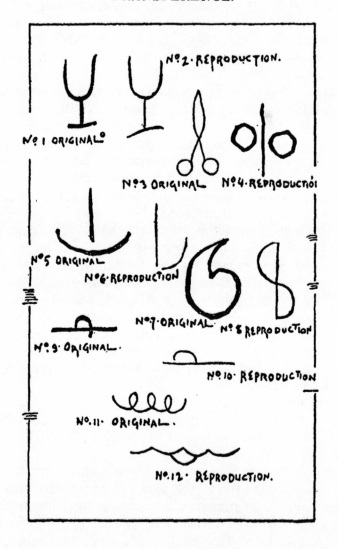

RESULTS OF EXPERIMENTS IN THOUGHT-TRANSFERENCE.

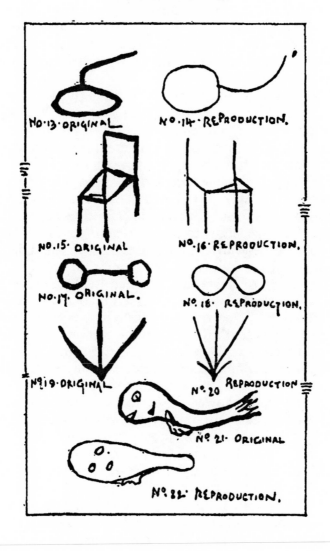

out of her range of vision had her eyes not been blind-folded.

The agent stopped looking at the drawing when the subject professed herself ready to make the attempt to reproduce it. The time occupied thus was from half a minute to two or three minutes. Then the handker-chief was removed, and she drew with a pencil what had occurred to her mind.

The reproductions were made generally without the agent following or watching the process. We repro-duce several of the attempts here, giving both the suc-cesses and the failures. Even the failures show the effect Mr. G. produced upon the reader's mind.

The experiments conducted so successfully in the family of the Rev. Mr. Creery, of Boston, and made public by Professor Barrett in *The Journal of Psy-chical Research,* show to what extent *Thought-Reading* may be successfully carried on in the quietude and confidence of a well-regulated family.

The mode of procedure adopted by Professor Bar-rett to test the faculty as possessed by the children was as follows: "One of the children," says Professor Barrett, "was sent into an adjoining room, the door of which I saw was closed. On returning to the sitting-room, and closing the door also, I thought upon some object in the house, fixed upon at random. Writing the name down, I showed it to the family present, the strictest silence being preserved throughout. We then all silently thought of the name of the thing selected. In a few seconds the door of the adjoining room was heard to open, and after a short interval the child would enter the sitting-room, generally speaking, with the object selected. No one was allowed to leave the sitting-room after the object had been fixed upon, and no communication with the child was conceivable, as her place was often changed. Further, the only in-structions given to the child were to fetch some object in the house that I would think upon and, together with the family, silently keep in mind, to the exclusion as far as possible of all other ideas."

Now, if Professor Barrett had told the children to select a word, and upon coming into the room were to spell or state what the word was, I question if the experiments would have been so successful. The articles thought of, whether a hair brush, an orange, wine glass, apple, or a playing card, were of such a nature that a definite picture or image of the thing thought of could be formed in the mind. The father, mother, and even Professor Barrett, seem to have been especially in *rapport* with the little sensitives, and thus all the more readily were they able to transmit the mental picture of the articles selected. Trick or collusion in this case is absolutely out of the question. It would be interesting to know if these young sensitives, who were so bright in 1881, still retain, or have increased or lost, their powers.

There were 312 trials made during Professor Barrett's stay of six days, who adds—"One most striking piece of success, when the things selected were divulged to none of the family, was five cards running named correctly on the first trial—the odds against this happening once in our series, being considerably over one million to one. We had altogether a good many similar batches, the two longest runs being eight consecutive successes, once with cards and once with names, when the adverse odds in the former cases were over one hundred and forty-two millions to one and on the latter, something incalculably greater. *Walls and closed doors made no difference."*

Something after the foregoing style are drawing-room entertainments given. If failure result, no one is blamed, and ridiculous mistakes only lend pleasure to the company, where all are known one to the other. The usual method is to select someone for *Thought-*

Reader. Lady or gentleman, matters little. He or she is sent out of the room. Some one in the room generally takes the lead, who may suggest the article to be selected and hidden, which the thought-reader is to find. The article selected is thought of by the entire company. The reader is to go to the place where it is, lift it, put it down, or give it to some one else; or to find a certain book and remove it from its place on table or elsewhere, and put it somewhere else; to come in and sit on a certain chair, or to lead someone else to it, or perform whatever other test that is decided upon. The reader is admitted into the room, and, if at all receptive, will do or say something like what is desired—often going direct to the spot, lifting the article, or doing the things which the company have decided upon.

A good plan is to get the assistance of one or two friends, use a bag of counters, upon which numbers 10 to 100 are placed; also a smaller bag with numbers 1 to 9. Let the sensitive sit at a table in such a position, so as, if not blind-folded, he or she could not see what the agent has in his hand. Use the small bag to begin with. Let one friend hold the bag, another select a number. When both have carefully looked at it let it be handed to the agent, who shall fix his eyes steadily upon the figure, and picture the said figure in his mind. The sensitive will in one or two minutes either say or write down what the figure is. If these experiments become satisfactory, the larger bag can be used. The experiments with numbers must not be continued too long, and so weary the faculty. In the same way a number of simple outline designs can be used—these presented one by one to the agent or operater—a fish, a boy and barrow, a fireman with escape, a negro and banjo, a lecturer on platform, an orange, a book, etc., such as are found in children's school books; repeating the same processes as above. No one must speak but the agent and the percipient, nor is the agent to know what the numbers or designs are before the experiments are commenced.

Should failure occur, select another medium. In a company of twenty to thirty persons it will be very strange if a good thought-reading sensitive is not found. In which case, more serious experiments may be attempted subsequently, and attain scientific value.

The *Thought-Reader* should be blindfolded, and *resign* himself to the *influences* of the agent or operator. Although he understands that something is expected of him, he is not to be anxious about what, but simply *act* as he *feels* himself prompted.

In proportion as the sensitive is able to give up anxiety and desire, so will he be able to become a good reader.

The operator, or agent, must concentrate his mind upon what is required, and *will* the sensitive to do it. When two or more persons, or all in the room, *are* concentrating their minds upon the thing, object, or word, the sensitive may all the sooner be influenced; but I prefer that one person should be chosen as the operator, and all intended experiments be submitted to him.

The process is analogous to that of mesmerism. We see traces here of the influence of mind over mind. We see the operator determines and the subject performs, although it may not be very clear how thought is actually projected, or in what way it is received, other than already suggested.

Practice makes perfect in this as in other things. Success is proportionate to success. A reader showing a degree of susceptibility at first attempts will generally improve by subsequent efforts. In a similar way, operators will make headway with practice. Some operators and sensitives will be successful at first trial; others again have failed after repeated attempts.

Plenty of time should be given for all first attempts.
Let the operator, for instance, keep his mind thoroughly fixed on the object. Should the reader be going
away from it, let the agent strongly wish him to go
back, *touch* it, lift it, etc., as previously decided upon
by the company.

All sensitive persons are likely to make good
Thought-Readers; the less sensitive, muscle readers.

MUSCLE-READING ENTERTAINMENTS.

Thought-Transference, like *Clairvoyance,* is un-
equalled in power and manifestation, even with good
percipients, and cannot be turned on like, and with,
the evening gas, to enlighten and entertain. Hence
those enterprising entertainers, like Bishop and Cum-
berland, depended on "muscle-reading," and "backed-
up their show" with tricks, some of them so puerile
and barefaced that a third-rate conjuror would be
ashamed of them.

The general public, however, enjoyed these entertainments. They were something new, and, like
"angel's visits," were few and far between. Not only
so, but that wonderful combination, the general public, saw that these entertainments were patronised by
men of science, such as Carpenter, Beard, Hammond,
Baron Kelvin, and others deeply in love with strictly
materialistic hypothesis. They were also patronised
by "society." These entertainers undertook to read
thoughts and expose spiritualism; and as the dear public loves mystery, it went. But the dear public don't
like to be "taken in," hence these performances are
generally repeated—in the next town.

The following, reported from St. John's N. B.,
January 17, 1887, in the *Herald,* is a good illustration
of the psychic and muscular indications involved in an

experiment of this kind: "In a '*Mind-Reading*' performance on Saturday night, after several examples indoors, the 'reader,' a young man who belongs to this city, asked for an outdoor test. The party separated, one remaining with the reader, and hid a pin in the side of a little house used by the switchman of the New Brunswick Railway at Mill Street. In their travels they went over the new railway trestle, a most difficult journey. The reader was blindfolded, and one took his wrist, but at the trestle hesitated, fearing to venture, and was told by the reader to let go his wrist and place his hand on his head. The subject did so, and the reader went upon the trestle. Some of the party suggested that the bandage should be removed, but he told them not to mind, and, the subject again taking the wrist, he went over the ice and snow-covered sleepers. With a firm step he crossed to the long wharf, went over as far as the mill gates, then quickly turned, retraced his steps, and went back to the corner of Mill Street. Here he rested a minute, then again took the subject's hand, and in less than five minutes afterwards found the pin. At the conclusion of the test, the reader inquired what the matter had been when they first reached the trestle. It was easily explained. The storm had covered the sleepers with snow, and it was thought dangerous, even for a man not blindfolded to cross them. The subject felt anxious for the reader's safety, and hesitated about going across. The tests were most satisfactory. Thought or mind-reading applied to these experiments is a misnomer. If this young gentleman could 'read thoughts' by musculation, or *contact*, he would have known what the matter had been when they first reached the trestle. Muscle-reading is not thought-reading. Hence it is classified as spurious."

Any number of illustrations could be given of such entertainments. The foregoing is sufficiently adequate to give an idea of how these muscle (not thought) reading entertainments are given.

For drawing-room entertainments, first blindfold the reader, who is conducted out of the room while the experiments are decided upon. The blindfolding helps to mystify friends, who think the work is rendered more difficult. As a matter of fact, the reader's work is rendered much more easy. It helps to isolate him, and leaves his mind much less entrammelled by sights and impressions which would otherwise prevent him receiving *the* impressions which it is desirable he should receive.

Suppose the reader is to locate the seat of an imaginary pain, the assistant or operator *pro tem.* will grasp* with his left hand the sensitive's right wrist and hold it firmly. While the reader is endeavouring to locate the pain, the operator must give up his will, and think intently on the situation of the pain. The reader will then locate it.

There is less secret in this than appears at first sight. The sensitive, or reader, is simply guided or led by the operator, and the reader's hand either stops partially over or is pressed upon the seat of the pain. He then declares he has found the seat of the pain, and points it out accordingly.

A somewhat similar method is adopted in finding the pin, or the *hole* in which a pin *had been.* The racing and flying about of public *Thought-Readers* are only so much "theatrical side," thrown in to give dramatic effect to their performances.

In reading the numbers on bank-notes, or spelling out certain words, a board with the numerals and the alphabet (see front cover) is placed in sight of the audience. The reader takes the wrist of the operator, and, commencing at the left side of the board, pro-

---

* The *contact* is usually made by the agent taking the wrist, or by placing his hand on the brow of the reader.

ceeds from figure to figure till he detects the right one. The operator thinks only of *one* figure or letter at a time. This is the whole secret of "musculation." Even when the operators are sincere, and are careful to give no conscious indications to the reader, yet it is almost certain, if they keep their mind fixed on the desired figure or letter, object or place, they will unconsciously indicate to the reader the right number or letter.

To find an article, number, or do a certain act, it is necessary for the reader to give prompt obedience to the indications given him. The concentration of attention necessary can only come with practice. No end of surprises and amusement will follow if the operator honestly concentrates his mind upon the things to be done, and a good muscle-reader is found to take up the indications. Apparently, the most difficult feats are sometimes accomplished.

During the experiments, the reader will have curious sensations, such as heaviness of feeling, dread and uncertainty, and then *blankness* of mind, followed by an impulse to do something. If the reader can keep his mind passive enough, he may receive impressions, as in thought-transference; anyway, it is advisable to wait for the impulse to move and to do. *The highest percentages of success always follow.*

General directions for the cultivation of experimental *Thought-Transference* and *Mind-Reading* given in these pages are sufficiently specific to be found thoroughly practical by those who have put them into practice; and certainly no harm, either mental or physical, can come to those who are willing to give them a fair trial.

CHAPTER VII.

SPIRITUALISM.

Any reference to *Spiritualism* here will be dealt with in the light of the preceding chapters.

It has been established on the clearest evidence that *Thought-Transference* and reception between two nearly harmonised or sympathetic human beings, or embodied human spirits, are possible, and this without intermediate sense or physical agencies. If, then, between mind and mind on earth, distance or space being no obstacle, matter no hindrance, why not between mind disincarnate—if the reader can conceive of mind apart from the human brain and organism—and mind incarnate? *If not, why not?*

It seems to me very difficult, if we accept the first, to reject the latter conclusion. If we accept the latter, we are committed in the main to belief in *Spiritualism,* ancient and modern. If we admit that it is possible for a disembodied spirit to communicate with us in *dream, vision,* or, as in the case of Miss Howett, have our hands influenced to write, or that we see and converse with spirits, as in the case of Mary Reynolds, we then admit, and accept in the main, the essential features of what is known as *Spiritualism.* The subject is not only interesting, but of vital importance; therefore, I think, the fear of being called a *"Spiritualist,"* or any other name, should not prevent us sounding to the depths the psychic possibilities of the human soul.

THE AUTO-TRANCE.

THE SPIRIT WITHIN US.

There is *Spiritualism and Spiritualism*. That which I am most interested in is not so much a hankering after *spirits*, "*spirit controls*," and the phenomena, generally recognised as the right thing in certain circles, as that other *Spiritualism* which leads to an honest endeavour on our parts to ascertain if we are spirits, here and now, albeit clothed for the time being in an organic envelope, relating us to our present estate.

If we are embodied spirits, it will be possible for the spirit-man (the essential self—*ego, I am*), in each human being to communicate at times, and under certain fitting conditions, with other fellow-beings, under such circumstances, and in such a way, as to make it clear :—

(*a.*) *That the communications could not have been transmitted and received by the ordinary channels, or physical sense organs, which in ordinary circumstances appear essential to our exchange of thought.*

(*b.*) *That the exchange of thought, in independence of the ordinary sense channels, will demonstrate that man must possess other, extraordinary or psychic, organs for the transmission and the reception of thought.*

Both positions I have endeavoured to sustain on the foregoing pages; and, lastly, concerning *Spiritualism*, I have arrived at the profound conclusion that spirit-communion—that is, *Thought-Transmission*, from the disembodied to the embodied—*is a solemn fact*. After carefully eliminating all the possibilities of self-deception—auto-trance, discreet degrees of consciousness, of natural and acquired *Clairvoyance*, of *Thought-Transference*, and *Mind-Reading*, and lastly, the puerile performances of conjurors and the simulated phenomena of tricksters—*there remains evidence of disembodied or disincarnate spirit, and of such control influencing and directing the actions of men, just as one man in this life influences and directs the actions of another.*

What I esteem, however, as satisfactory evidence might not be evidence to another; and I for one do not think it necessary to open up the life chambers of my psychic experiences to the indifferent, the thoughtless, or the sceptic, to furnish the desired evidence. *Others must travel by the way I have come to understand something of that way.* All men cannot believe alike, hence it will not be surprising that some will accept as sufficient evidence of spirit what others would deem insufficient.

It is not my intention meantime to advocate *Spiritualism.* I only refer to it, in so far as it is related to *'Clairvoyance and Thought-Transference."* However, *Phenomenal Spiritualism* is not a matter of belief so much as of evidence, and many eminent thinkers have been compelled by the force of the evidence to accept SPIRITUALISM now, who, a quarter of a century ago, would have hesitated, principally through fear of ridicule, to speak of the subject in language of ordinary civility.

While I am convinced that such communications be-:ween the so-called dead and the living are possible, I do not know and feel satisfied that much which is accepted as evidence of the existence and influence of spirits by the majority of the unthinking and excitable crowd who rush after novelties, and perchance call themselves *"spiritualists,"* is traceable to no other or higher source than our own innate, but little understood, human or psychic powers. I have arrived at this conclusion also, as the result of carefully investigating spiritualism, and it is therefore not an *a priori* hypothesis conveniently elaborated from my own or borrowed from the brains of others who are opponents of *Spir-*

itualism. It is probable, had I not devoted the greater part of my life to Hindu *Spiritualism,* as one of the factors in human character, I should have known but little of that sympathetic transference of thought from one mind to another, or of the light which that fact throws upon our dual or compound existence.

In this *"sympathetic transference of thought"* we find a solution to the problem of *Spiritualism,* whether old or new. I conclude, with the *Hindu Adepts,* "The true springs of our organisation are *not* these muscles, these veins, these arteries, which are described with so much exactness and care. There exist in organised bodies *internal occult forces* which do not follow the gross mechanical laws we imagine, and to which we would reduce everything." Or, as the *High-Grade Adepts* put it more strongly—"Beyond the limits of this visible anatomy commences another anatomy, whose phenomena we cannot perceive; beyond the limits of this external physiology of forces, of action, and of motion, exists another *invisible physiology, whose principles, effects, and laws are of the greatest importance to know."*

It may be esteemed reprehensible to *"seek communion with the dead,"* but to know ourselves, to fathom this *invisible physiology,* whose principles, effects, and laws are of such importance to understand, I hold to be not only legitimate but perfectly laudable. How can we serve God (*Nature*), whom we have not seen, *if we do not understand ourselves,* whom we think we have seen, or the laws which govern our being, as created by *Nature? To know ourselves as we should, we ought not to neglect the search for "the spirit within us."*

THE REJECTION OF THE PSYCHIC.

Many persons—scientific, theological, learned, and illiterate—reject the psychic, and refrain from investigating, either from constitutional bias or from crass ignorance; and such have played the part of learned Sadducees or low fellows of the baser sort before anything having the remotest flavor of spirit. The man of science is rendered purblind by *"my hypothesis,"* the theologian by *"my belief,"* the man of the world by *"my business,"* or *"my position."* The respectable church-goer—who vaccinates his children, as he has them baptised, because it is the proper thing to do— *has neither the head nor heart, apparently, to understand anything beyond the common material ideas of the hour.* He would crucify all new thought, or new *Spiritualism* for that matter, as the Jews did *Jesus,* the *Master,* because the new doctrines promulgated and the new wonders performed tend to subvert the present respectable order of things.

The worship of *Diana* is not confined to ancient *Ephesus.* The great *Diana* of old was the type of that "Respectable Custom" which the majority of mankind worship and obey to-day, because, as of yore, it conserves their vested interests, official connections, and brings them *"much gain."* As for the man in the street—the multitude having no shepherd—he is always more or less hypnotised by the well-clad and well-fed, smug-faced worshippers of the aforesaid "Respectable Custom;" hence he is ever ready to shout *"Crucify,"* or *"Hurrah,"* or aught else he is influenced to do, especially if such exercises give him pleasure and excitement for the time being. He accepts or rejects as he sees "his betters" think best, and so, unfortunately, is unfitted to a large degree for the intelligent investigation of his own nature. These form the largest group of rejectors of the phenomenal evidences of soul.

The psychic, however, has suffered less from such rejectors than from those who claim to be recognised and known as converts and exponents of the same,

who at best have only shown themselves to be *"seekers
after a sign."* They may have run into the wilder-
ness and have had a bit of miraculous bread, and yet
not be a pennyworth the better of it in either soul
or body—*i.e.,* life or conduct. These, by their foolish-
ness, have prevented many well-meaning and otherwise able persons investigating the psychic, for the
latter saw nothing in the lives of professed *Spiritualists*
to make them desire to have anything to do with *Spiritualism.* Moreover, coming in contact with the *icono-
clastic* western *Spiritualism* as it is carried on in
Europe and America, they have become disgusted with
the crude and the coarse therein, as they have with the
revelations, inspirations, and fads, advocated by certain so-called mediums and Clairvoyants; and hence
have rejected the wheat because of the apparent great
quantity of tares.

The Fraudulent In Spiritualism.

I am afraid the trend of modern civilisation, which
leads men from the beauties and quietude of hill and
dale, of valley and river side, into crowded city life,
has tended to make men *exoteric. They run after
signs and wonders without, and too little to the spirit
within.* The broader view of being, and that self-
culture and purity which arises from the exercise of
man's innate powers, and makes for true regeneration
and spiritual progress, here and hereafter, have been
more or less sacrificed to the external and the phenomenal.

The love of the phenomenal, in and out of western
Spiritualism, has created a crowd of harpies, impos-
tors, or fraudulent mediums—male and female—who
trade on human credulity, some to earn a pittance,
and others to gratify vanity. Men and women have
been known to risk reputation for both. *In this way*

Spiritualism has its quota of deceivers and deceived.
There are some people who must have phenomena,
just as there are other people who will have sermons.
If they don't get exactly what they want, they with-
draw "their patronage"—the finances. So, if the patronage is to be retained, phenomena and sermons have
to be supplied—*if the first are fraudulent or the latter
stolen.*

Seeing how fugitive real psychological phenomena
are—natural or induced—one must necessarily hesitate to accept so-called "trance addresses," "inspirational orations," "medical controls," clairvoyant and
second-sight exhibitions, *which are supplied to order,
to gratify patrons, at so much per hour.* It is human
to err, but the manufacturer of spurious phenomena,
the impostor who trades on the ties, and the dearest
of human affections, is a devil. There is no iniquity
too low—earthly or devilish—to which he will not as
readily descend to gratify his vampirish nature.

I am not disposed to accept the infallibility of spirits
for that of Popes—large or small—or professional
media, in place of professional priests and ministers,
*and there is by far too much of this in the western
Spiritualism of to-day.*

In the foregoing connection, I must refer to another
source of error—this time, however, more related to
physical rather than psychic phenomena—viz., the
credulity of those who are disposed to believe that
certain conjurors are aided in their performances by
spirit agency. Personally, I would sooner believe that
mediums for "Physical Phenomena" resorted to con-
juring to aid "*spirits*," than believe that "*spirits*" resorted to "hanky-panky" to aid conjurors. No wonder "frauds" smile. Years ago I had to protest against
this absurdity, when people—who ought to know better—talked this kind of nonsense about conjurors, as
they do about certain fraudulent mediums now—viz.,

"they are aided by spirits." Owing to this lack of discrimination and want of trained discernment in *Spiritualists* and the general public, mediumistic frauds have fooled, to their utmost bent, fresh groups of dupes at home and abroad.

I am none the less disposed to accept the genuine, because we recognise sources of error connected therewith, *and are determined to set our faces against palpable frauds.*

SPIRITUALISM WITHOUT SPIRITS.

I will now turn from the wretched arena of imposture, duplicity, and credulity, *to the genuine,* but little understood, phenomena in *Spiritualism.* The student has been taught in this book that much which has been attributed to the agency of disembodied spirits is due, in many instances, *to the action of man's own psychic states, "the double, who is wiser than he,"* and to the fact that, as often as not, trance states, automatic and planchette writing, *are self-induced conditions.* Equally so, *Clairvoyance, Thought-Transference,* and *Psychometry* do not require the "agency of spirit" to account for their existence as "gifts," qualities or powers. It will be time enough to admit such agency —*that of disembodied spirits*—when the evidence in each particular case is reasonably conclusive. *I think this is the only wise and safe course to pursue.*

Clairvoyance may be *natural or induced, self-cultivated or cultivated by aid of a mesmerist.* As it has been exercised naturally, and without any such aid, the exhibition of *Clairvoyance*—in itself—is no evidence of disembodied spirit-presence or control. Equally, the seeing of, and the describing of, spirits by a *Clairvoyant*—even if the descriptions are apparently accurate—*may present no evidence of the real presence of such spirits.* I do not deny that *Clair-*

voyants can see spirits, but the mere fact of being able to see and describe spirits, is not sufficient evidence— the *seer* is controlled by spirit-power to see, or that the spirits described are actually *bona-fide* spirits. Frequently, so-called spirits have no other existence than the image of them possessed by some positive-minded individual. A *Clairvoyant, perceiving* these images, might naturally enough conclude she was actually seeing the spirits which she described.

If Mr. Stead, for instance, is convinced that "Sister Dora," "*Cardinal Manning*," or "*Lord Tennyson*," are at his side, in his rooms, influencing and directing his mind, or at other times actually controlling his arm and hand to write, a *Clairvoyant* in sympathy with him may describe this or that other spirit he is *thinking* about. But that does not prove the spirit or spirits are actually present.

A lady (Mrs. Davis), whose name has come prominently before the public as Mr. Stead's *Clairvoyante*, being questioned as to Mr. Stead's automatic writing and her own gift, said:—"I know probably more about that than anyone. I was in his office some time in the beginning of December last regarding the forthcoming publication of a book of mine concerning *Spiritualism*. The conversation turned upon spiritualistic automatic handwriting. I did not know the deceased lady who was writing through him, but I saw her behind his chair as distinctly as if she had been in the flesh. I described her position as she stood and her appearance. She at once wrote through Mr. Stead's hand confirming all I had stated concerning her in my description. Mr. Stead's hand continued to write. I knew afterwards it wrote out a message stating that another spirit was in the room. Mr. Stead asked me if I could describe that spirit. I had to wait some little time before I detected it, and there I recognised as in the flesh a very famous personage recently dead, whose loss was mourned all the world over in prose and verse. I carefully described the spirit as he appeared to me, and then Mr. Stead said I was right. But, I answered, I see another male spirit. Ask the deceased lady who is writing through you to write the name of the last spirit. Mr. Stead's hand automatically moved, and he wrote the name of a son of the famous personage already alluded to." Mrs. Davis says she has been strongly impressed with the fact that Mr. Stead has been selected by the spirits as their champion from the peculiar and unique position he occupies in the journalistic world, and he will be the agent who will break through the solid walls of bigotry and prejudice. Mr. Stead may or may not have written under spirit influence, and this lady may or may not have seen spirits as described. We must not conclude in the latter case that Mr. Stead and his "trustworthy clairvoyante" are stating anything they do not believe to be true. I believe she saw, as described or thought of by Mr. Stead, a "deceased lady;" and that she also saw, as equally thought by him, "a very famous personage recently dead;" also "another male spirit," whose name she did not know until Mr. Stead wrote the name. This narrative, however interesting as to automatic writing and spirit agency in the opinions of those concerned, conveys no tangible evidence of either the one or the other. To us it is interesting in the fact that Mrs. Davis *saw the spirits thought of by Mr. Stead.* We must think twice before we can accept this as evidence of spirits and spirit-presence. Although it is possible those concerned have evidence, we have not. We have, however, evidence here of *Thought-Transmission* and psychic impressionability.

When we read of persons who have been raised up, as mediums of *St. Peter, St. Paul,* or *St. John,* or a publishing company being run by Shakespeare through a special medium, and worked by a syndicate of *Spir-*

itualists, I think we are entitled to doubt these claims, even though a dozen clairvoyants vouched for the existence and presence of the aforesaid spirits.

Psychometry furnishes evidence that many so-called spirits *are not spirit* "at all, at all"—only visions of the originals; and the fact that such and such an individual has been accurately described—actions and manners carefully indicated—and this has been and is accurately done in health and disease daily—is no evidence, in itself, that *Psychometers* have seen spirits. Thus, when a *Psychometer* places a geological specimen to his forehead, and describes an *"antediluvian monster,"* roaring and walking about, no one but a very shallow individual would imagine for a second the *Psychometer* was actually seeing the original. So many of the spirits and spectres seen do not proceed from our own brains, but from objects, relics, and old houses, which had been in times past impinged by the living presence and magnetism of the originals. Then we must take into consideration those spectres which proceed from our own minds, such as the realistic images which are sometimes projected from the background of consciousness to our eyes and ears. Many so-called spirits are simply the product of diseased neurological conditions, in short, *hallucinations,* which arise from some derangement of the optic and auditory centres. The spectres seen by *Nicolai* gradually disappeared as he lost blood, as the prescribed leeches tranquilised his system. We have no reason to believe the spectres he saw, visions and what not, were actually either spirits or produced by spirits.

Mind-Reading In Spiritualism.

Mind-Reading is the commonest of most common experiences. I have known mediums to graphically describe scenes, persons, and incidents with such vividness as to impress one they must be controlled by

spirits intimately acquainted with the whole circumstances which were revealed. *Closer examination indicates that all the information so given by these mediums was based on the thought-read phase. That is,
the information was culled from the minds of spirits
in the flesh, and did not come from disembodied
sources.*

Some years ago I attended a series of seances in
Liverpool. Nearly all the family were mediums of
some sort. I was at this time very critical in my investigations. Consequently, the following incident was
not lost upon me. One evening the circle met, with
the usual members. Shortly after the circle was
formed, the daughter of the house went into the *trance*
state. There were several controls, one of whom
professed to be a man who, the day before, had been
injured on board one of *Lambert & Holt's* steamers,
which lay in the *Bramley Moore Dock.* The *"spirit"*
described the accident, how he was injured, and that
he was carried to the hospital, and had *"passed away."*
Owing to the suddenness of his death, he wished us
to communicate with his family, and desired the circle
to pray for him, etc. As near as I can recollect, when
asked for further particulars, name, family, there was
no definite reply. The medium quivered, and a new
control had taken possession of her. I, however,
neither doubted the *bona-fides* of the spirit nor the
medium. I was especially interested in this control.
I thought this time I had obtained a test of spirit
identity. But alas for the imperfection of human
hopes, I was doomed to disappointment. I clung to
the idea the spirit would come back again, and when
he got "more power," we would get the particulars
he wanted to give us. He did not come back—and no
wonder. Four months subsequently, I met the real
Simon Pure in the flesh.

To explain more fully: On the day previous to the

seance mentioned, I was on board the newly-arrived steamer in question. The lumpers were getting out the cargo. This man had ben working on the top of the cargo in the main hold *"hooking on."* I paid no particular attention at the time to him, but an hour after I heard a great outcry, and saw a rush of men to the main hold. When I turned back and got there, I found this man senseless and bleeding.

The hooks had slipped off a bale while easing out some cargo. One of them had caught the poor fellow in the mouth, and had torn up his cheek almost to the right ear. He was to all appearance dying. I temporarily dressed his face, and the stevedore had him put on a stretcher and sent to the hospital. *I did not know his name or the hospital to which he was removed.* That day and the next the whole scene was vividly impressed on my mind. Hence that night the circumstances at the seance seem to me to be quite natural. Everything advanced was wonderfully apposite and convincing. It was not till I saw the man, and conversed with him, that my so-called test of spirit identity resolved itself into so much thought or *Mind reading,* so that, even presuming the medium or sensitive was controlled by *"a spirit,"* there can be no doubt the source of the spirit's information was purely mundane.

Automatic and planchette writing, upon which so much reliance is placed, as furnishing evidence of *"disembodied spirit control,"* presents similar difficulties. The recording of forgotten incidents, and predicting possibilities in the future, are not beyond the powers of the innate human spirit—wholly and utterly unaided by spirit agency. Therefore automatic writing —when genuine—*does not necessarily furnish evidence of spirit control, not even when the person who writes believes, and honestly believes too, he is so controlled to write.*

CHAPTER VIII.

PHENOMENAL SPIRITUALISM.

Automatic writing is a phase of *Phenomenal Spiritualism* most difficult to prove. In the majority of cases we are reduced to the awkward position of accepting or rejecting the assertions of the persons who declare that the writing done by them is automatic— that is, written without thought and volition on their part. A close examination of this claim may lead to the conclusion that automatic writing is not impossible. Whether the controlling agent is *"the spirit within us," or a disembodied spirit, or both, is not a matter of much importance, if it is established, the writing is automatic.* When messages are written without volition, in the handwriting of deceased persons, signed by their names, such messages must be treated on their merits. I have seen messages written in this way. I have seen messages written, not only automatically, but *direct.* Some were written the reverse way, and could only be read by holding up to the light or to a mirror. The direct writing was done in an exceedingly short time, two or three hundred words in less time than an expert stenographer could write the same by the most expeditious efforts. The evidence in favor of *Telepathic* writing is not very strong, but of *direct* writing there appears to be abundant proof.

Dr. Nichols, in his fascinating work, *"Forty Years Of American Life,"* writes;—"I knew a Methodist sailor in New York, a simple, illiterate, earnest man, who became what is called a test medium. He came to see me in *Cincinnati,* and one evening we had also as visitors two distinguished lawyers: one of them a brother of *Major Anderson*, "the hero of *Fort Sumter*;" the other, a gentleman from *Michigan*, and one of the ablest lawyers practising in the *Supreme Court of the United States.* I had brought into the drawing-room a heavy walnut table, and placed it in the centre of the room. The medium sat down on one side of it, and the sharp *Michigan* lawyer, who was a stranger to us and the medium, on the other. The medium placed his fingers lightly upon the table. It tilted up under them, the two legs nearest him rising several inches. The lawyer examined the table, and tried to give it a similar movement, but without success. There was a force and a consequent movement he could not account for. There was no other person near the table, there was no perceptible muscular movement, and in no way in which it could be applied to produce the effect.

"When there was no doubt on this point, the lawyer, at the suggestion of the medium, wrote with careful secrecy on five bits of paper—rolling each up like a pea as he wrote—the names of five deceased persons whom he had known. Then he rolled them about until he felt sure that no one could tell one pellet from the other. Then, pointing to them successively, the tipping table selected one, which the gentleman, without opening, put in his waistcoat pocket, and threw the rest into the fire.

"The next step was to write the ages of these five persons at their death, on as many bits of paper, which were folded with the same care. One of these was selected, and again, without being opened, deposited in the lawyer's pocket, which now contained a name and a number indicating age.

"With the same precautions the lawyer then wrote, in the same way, on bits of paper, the places where these persons died, the diseases of which they died, and the dates of their decease, going through the same process with each. He had then in his pocket five little balls of paper, each selected by a movement of the table, for which no one could account.

"At this moment the hand of the medium seized a pencil, and with singular rapidity dashed off a few lines, addressed to the lawyer as from a near relative, and signed with a name which the medium very certainly had never heard.

"The lawyer, very much astonished, took from his pocket the five paper balls, unrolled them, spread them before him on the table, and read the same name as the one on the written message, with the person's age, the place and time of death, and the disease of which he died. They all corresponded with each other and the message. No person had approached the table, and neither lawyer nor medium had moved. It was in my own house, under a full gas light, and, so far as I could see, or can see now, no deception was possible.

"The written communication, which purported to come from a deceased relative of the gentleman, only expressed, in affectionate terms, the happiness at being able to give him this evidence of immortality."

This incident is introduced here in illustration of one out of many phases of mediumship known to Spiritualists. We see here both psychic and physical powers exercised, not generally recognised as possible. A massive table moved without physical leverage or exertion, and "Thoughts Read," which formed the basis of the message. Trickery and collusion in this instance are absolutely out of the question. The only questions which remain to answer are: "Did this medium possess in himself the powers referred to? or did he possess them in consequence of being controlled by a disembodied spirit, as claimed by the message?" Although the message in itself did not contain evidence of any other source of information than that emanating from the lawyer's own mind, we are forced to the conclusion that either the medium or the spirit controlling the medium had power to read his mind, and of exerting what *Professor Crookes* and *Sergeant Cox* would call *Psychic Force* to move the table, and indicate what pellets to select. *We have here evidence of an intelligence capable of exercising an unknown force and of reading thoughts—that intelligence claimed to be a human spirit.*

TRANCE ADDRESSES.

Trance and inspirational addresses, however, do not, in my opinion, furnish much evidence of the reality of spirit control. We are interested in the phenomena —taking for granted that these trance and inspirational states are genuine—although the evidence of external spirit control presented is often *nil.* The controls may or may not be veritable realities to their own mediums—professional or otherwise—but this is of little value, as evidence, to the public. I have known mediumistic and otherwise sensitive persons to be controlled—*i.e.,* taken possession of by their reading. One gentleman swallowed large doses of Theodore Parker. In time he thought of Parker, talked of Parker, and finally believed he was "inspired" by Theodore Parker. This gentleman had been a Unitarian before being a Spiritualist, and doubtless his mind had been broadened and brightened by his course of Theodore Parker; but beyond his own belief and the evident state of excitability he exhibited when speaking under this supposed control, there was actually no evidence of "spirit control" worthy of notice.

Mrs. Cora L. V. Tappan-Richmond, an inspirational medium, from *America,* delivered a series of remarkable addresses in England about twenty years ago. These were published by J. Burns, of Southampton Row, Holborn, W. C. A young gentleman from

Brighton heard and read the lectures, and finally budded forth as "an inspirational speaker." For a long time the public got nothing but the Tappan lectures diluted. We had the same marvellous, even flow, similar processes of reasoning, fertility of illustration, and unbounded capacity for assertion. No one dare say this person was not inspired by the spirits. It might have been a way the spirits had of breaking in their instrument, but I had a shrewd suspicion the young orator was controlled by his reading. I don't know how many others have been influenced in this way. I have noticed when a noted medium "*came to town,*" delivered a number of addresses in public, or gave seances in private, immediately thereafter a number of imitators professed—correctly or otherwise—principally otherwise—to have been controlled by the guides, who were supposed to control the medium aforesaid, and that they would soon be able to give addresses and manifestations, and what not. On the other hand, the noted mediums averred "*their guides never controlled any other than themselves,*" etc. The conscientious investigator is left to wonder how much imitation, vanity, and self-deception have to do with such statements.

Some of the most perfect oratory and some of the ablest and most cogent lectures and addresses I have ever listened to have been given by trance and inspirational mediums. It was stated, as evidence of spirit control, by those who professed to know, "*that these mediums could not reason and speak that way in their normal condition.*" All of which is worthy of consideration. At the same time I saw nothing inherently impossible—judging from a physiological or cerebral-physiognomic standpoint—to prevent these persons delivering, unaided by spirit agency, the addresses referred to. That a person speaks with greater ability, intelligence, or fluency in the trance state compared with his known powers in the waking state, cannot alone, be accepted as proof of spirit control. I have seen hypnotised subjects do the same. But the reality, or otherwise, or spirit agency, cannot be estimated by the superiority, or otherwise, of the addresses and messages given.

In all public meetings and in seances where a medium is expected to give trance and inspirational addresses, the platform is *"supported"* or the chair surrounded by sympathisers, whose presence is esteemed favourable to *"good conditions"*—a *"nebulous term"* better understood by *Spiritualists* than the public. When the address is, as is often the case, a miserable jumble of things inconsequential, old, experienced *Spiritualists* say it is owing *"to bad conditions,"* i.e., the influence of the audience on the speaker being conflicting and bad, hence the inconclusive rambling of the spirit's oration. Whether this is the true explanation or not, whether the medium was really controlled or not, or the addresses successful or not, the fact remains that *Spiritualists* admit that the "message" is not only "seriously modified," according to the channel (or medium) through whom it is given, but that it may be deflected and distorted by the influences of the audience to whom it is given. *Whatever the real cause of the imperfect oratory, what is this but admitting the thoughts transferred from the audience to the sensitive either make or mar the utterance?* If spirit utterance is thus influenced, it becomes a difficult matter to decide how much of the original message has reached us as intended, and how unwise it is for some to have their lives directed by such uncertain counsel.

There are many persons so organised, that when they come in contact with *Spiritualism,* (not knowing anything about *Clairvoyance, Psychometry, Thought-Transference, Thought-Reading,* etc.,) are so convinced by what they hear and see for the first time—so much out of the ordinary run of their experience—the only way they can account for the phenomena is, "that they must be the work of spirits, for no human being could tell what they knew, or what they wanted, save a spirit who could read their thoughts." *This is just where, I think, the error creeps in.* Those very revelations which they in ignorance so readily attribute as only possible coming from disembodied spirits, may be and are in some instances quite possible to man, unaided by any such agency.

Many years ago I sat with *Mr. David Duguid,* the *Glasgow* painting medium. I had a *"direct spirit painting"* done. It was a correct—as far as I can recollect—painting of a small hotel and stead, in the North of *India,* where I as a child had been sent for my health. Neither Mr. Duguid nor the control claimed to possess any actual knowledge of me, or of the circumstances of my childhood. When I had an opportunity of attending the seance in question, I wondered if such a scene could be painted, and my wonder was greater when it was done.

Here again, we have evidence of *Thought-Transference.* Whether *Mr. Duguid,* by some *occult* power, caused the direct painting to be done—his own spirit doing it while his body was in the trance state—or the painting was produced by one of his controls, many may not believe. I am willing to state my belief that the painting was not done by Duguid, the medium, or any other person present in the room. One of the controls of the medium claimed to have painted the little sketch, and, truth to tell, it is not more difficult to accept this hypothesis than "the spirit of the medium did it." *In our ordinary experience of human nature, we do not find it usual for men to give credit to others—men or spirits—for what they are capable of doing and saying themselves.*

REFLECTIONS.

It is quite possible, seeing that out of this life into the next, through the PORTALS OF DEATH, pass all sorts and conditions of human beings, that in the next stage of existence—most closely allied to that in which we now live—mankind are not essentially different in character from what we find now. It is not, therefore, necessary to call in the agency of demons, as distinct from human spirits, to account for the phenomena of *Spiritualism*. If in artificial somnambulism and the phenomena of the psychic state the operating agent is an embodied human spirit, it is possible the same human spirit, albeit, disembodied, may still retain power to control or influence other human beings.

There is another and more serious matter for consideration, concerning which our investigations of *Spiritualism* have thrown little or no light—*Spirit Identity*. Not only do their friends depart and never return, and many have promised to do so. How far are they certain when spirits have returned? They may have been deceived by their own impulsiveness, anxiety, and desire to feel and to know that "they are not lost but gone before." Again, admitting the genuineness of physical phenomena, and conceding that all the communications are really made by disembodied spirits or intelligent beings like unto themselves, what proof do they possess that they are really what they represent themselves to be, or what they appear to be in spirit circles? "A bad or mischievous spirit may, for aught they knew, personate their friends, *penetrate their secrets,* and deceive them with false representations." *This is certainly worth thinking about. My object in writing is not to turn my readers against Spiritualism, but to get them to bring into the investigation judgment, not only to analyse evidence, but*

the capacity to "judge not according
but judge righteous judgment." It is
purpose to deal with the history, eth
phenomena of Spiritualism. That has v.
by others. I merely write to show that Spirituam...
"has something in it," and is of such importance that
it is neither to be lightly rejected on the one hand, nor
are its phenomena at all times to be attributed to agency
of disembodied spirits.

Western Spiritualism is a many-sided subject, and too vast in its proportions to be dealt with here, and while I have no doubt that its public mediumistic exponents are no more perfect than the rest of humanity— much is laid at their door which may have a basis on fact—yet I do think they often suffer unjustly. Firstly, from the cries of the ignorant—educated or otherwise, matters little—who charge them with fraud, simply because such people are ignorant of the psychic possibilities of man; and, secondly, from the admiring and thoughtless many who are prepared to accept the commonest of psychic phases instanter as evidence of *"disembodied spirit"* presence and power. I have no doubt many phenomena are quite explicable on natural grounds. Setting aside the possibilities of self-deception in untrained observers, and of fraud in dishonest mediums, and of genuine phenomena traceable to the powers of the *"spirit which is within each of us,"* ere remains, to my mind, abundant evidence of the existence of *"discarnate spirit,"* possessing all the attributes of the human spirit, as we know ourselves from the study of man as a psychological subject. Unfortunately, the very best evidence in favor of both *"embodied"* and *"disembodied spirit"* is not of that kind which is available for publicity, for it is only taught the *Adepts* in the *Temples* of *India.* Still, I hold, if there is evidence (psychological and physical) for disembodied spirit in Western *Spiritualism,* I am also satisfied there is abundant evidence for embodied spirit in the psychological experiences of life, apart from what we know of *Spiritualism.*

I may fitly close these reflections by quoting the testimony of that keen scientific observer anent PHE-NOMENAL *Spiritualism*—namely, *Cromwell F. Varley, Esq., F.R.S.:*—"Twenty-five years ago I was a hard-headed unbeliever. . . . *Spiritual* phenomena, however, suddenly and quite unexpectedly was soon after developed in my own family. . . . This led me to inquire, and to try numerous experiments in such a way as to preclude, as much as circumstances would permit, the possibility of trickery and self-deception." . . . He then details various phases of the phenomena which had come within the range of his personal experience, and continues:—"Other and curious phenomena had occurred, proving the existence (*a*) of forces unknown to science; (*b*) *the power of instantly reading my thoughts;* (*c*) the presence of some intelligence or intelligences controlling these powers. . . . That the phenomena occur there is overwhelming evidence, and it is too late to deny their existence."

THE BIBLIOGRAPHY OF SPIRITUALISM is somewhat extensive. What books are best to recommend to beginners is not any easy matter to decide. *"THE BOOK OF DEATH, SOUL TRANSITION, HINDU SPIRITISM AND SOUL REINCARNA-*

TION, however, will repay perusal, and from the intellectual fitness, high moral tone, and spotless reputation of this book it may be safely recommended to all readers.

THE END.

COSIMO is a specialty publisher of books and publications that inspire, inform, and engage readers. Our mission is to offer unique books to niche audiences around the world.

COSIMO BOOKS publishes books and publications for innovative authors, nonprofit organizations, and businesses. **COSIMO BOOKS** specializes in bringing books back into print, publishing new books quickly and effectively, and making these publications available to readers around the world.

COSIMO CLASSICS offers a collection of distinctive titles by the great authors and thinkers throughout the ages. At **COSIMO CLASSICS** timeless works find new life as affordable books, covering a variety of subjects including: Business, Economics, History, Personal Development, Philosophy, Religion & Spirituality, and much more!

COSIMO REPORTS publishes public reports that affect your world, from global trends to the economy, and from health to geopolitics.

FOR MORE INFORMATION CONTACT US AT
INFO@COSIMOBOOKS.COM

* if you are a book lover interested in our current catalog of books

* if you represent a bookstore, book club, or anyone else interested in special discounts for bulk purchases

* if you are an author who wants to get published

* if you represent an organization or business seeking to publish books and other publications for your members, donors, or customers.

COSIMO BOOKS ARE ALWAYS AVAILABLE AT ONLINE BOOKSTORES

VISIT COSIMOBOOKS.COM
BE INSPIRED, BE INFORMED